How Your Congregation Learns

How Your Congregation Learns

The Learning Journey from Challenge to Achievement

Tim Shapiro

An Alban Institute Book

ROWMAN & LITTLEFIELD
Lanham • Boulder • New York • London

Published by Rowman & Littlefield
A wholly owned subsidiary of
The Rowman & Littlefield Publishing Group, Inc.
4501 Forbes Boulevard, Suite 200, Lanham, Maryland 20706
https://rowman.com

Unit A, Whitacre Mews, 26-34 Stannary Street, London SE11 4AB,
United Kingdom

Unless otherwise noted, all Scripture quotations are from the New Revised Standard Version of the Bible, copyright © 1989, Division of Christian Education of the National Council of the Church of Christ in the United States of American, and are used by permission.

Credit: William Stafford, excerpt from "A Ritual to Read to Each Other" from *Ask Me: 100 Essential Poems*. Copyright © 1960, 1998, 2014 by William Stafford and the Estate of William Stafford. Reprinted with the permission of The Permissions Company, Inc. on behalf of Graywolf Press, Minneapolis, Minnesota, www.graywolfpress.org.

Excerpt from the lyrics of "There's Always More," a song that appears on Glen Phillips's album *Swallowed by the New* is used with permission from Mr. Phillips's management.

British Library Cataloguing in Publication Information Available

Library of Congress Cataloging-in-Publication Data

Names: Shapiro, Tim, author.
Title: How your congregation learns : the learning journey from challenge to
  achievement / Tim Shapiro.
Description: Lanham : Rowman & Littlefield, a wholly owned subsidiary of The
  Rowman & Littlefield Publishing Group, Inc., [2017] | Includes
  bibliographical references and index.
Identifiers: LCCN 2017004179 (print) | LCCN 2017019602 (ebook) | ISBN
  9781566997454 (Electronic) | ISBN 9781566997768 (cloth : alk. paper) |
  ISBN 9781566997447 (pbk. : alk. paper)
Subjects: LCSH: Church renewal. | Change--Religious aspects--Christianity.
Classification: LCC BV600.3 (ebook) | LCC BV600.3 .S474 2017 (print) | DDC
  253--dc23
LC record available at https://lccn.loc.gov/2017004179

♾ ™ The paper used in this publication meets the minimum requirements of American National Standard for Information Sciences Permanence of Paper for Printed Library Materials, ANSI/NISO Z39.48-1992.

Printed in the United States of America

Contents

Acknowledgments

The most resilient learning takes place through relationships. This is true in congregations and other realms of life. So, I want to acknowledge people from whom I've learned.

I offer thanks to the congregations served by the Indianapolis Center for Congregations, its offices around the state, and the Congregational Resource Guide (http://www.thecrg.org). Particularly I want to thank a group of leaders that helped me understand the learning dynamics in the congregations they serve. This group includes Thomas Bartley, Lori Bievenour, Mary Cartwright, Helen Hempfling, Mark Knowles, Anne Marshall, Rebecca Ferrell Nickel, Lisa Schubert Nowling, Teri Thomas, Shelly Wood, Martin Wright, and Anastassia Zinke.

The Center for Congregations staff is a remarkable learning community that is deeply dedicated to its mission to strengthen congregations. I am grateful for Nancy Armstrong, Eunita Booker, Terrance Bridges, Matt Burke, Sofia Cook, Catharine Green, Carol Delph, Nancy DeMott, Kara Brinkerhoff Faris, Doug Hanner, Jerri Kinder, Katie Lindberg, Jane Mastin, Wendy McCormick, Kelly Minas, Aaron Spiegel, Rose Villaruel, Sue Weber, and Kate White.

I am grateful to Richard Bass for his encouragement regarding early thinking about the book.

I am appreciative of the time Sandra Herron, Alice Mann, and Gil Rendle took to talk about the learning journey.

A few sections of the book were previously published in various Alban Institute print and online publications. I am thankful to Dave Odom at Alban at Duke Divinity School for permission to present this material in slightly different form. Alban at Duke Divinity School, Leadership Education at Duke Divinity, the Faith and Leadership website (https://www.

faithandleadership.com) all contribute in numerous, positive ways to the formation of Christian leaders, including congregational leaders.

The work of the Center for Congregations is funded by Lilly Endowment, Inc. Their support is so comprehensive and tangible that it is difficult to find the right words to say "thank you." Program Officer John Wimmer is the founding director of the Indianapolis Center for Congregations. His positive contribution informs our work every day. Chris Coble serves as Vice President of Religion at Lilly Endowment. Additionally, the Lilly Endowment Religion program officers also include Jessicah Duckworth, Chanon Ross, and Brian Williams. Thank you for your support.

The Center's work is governed by its Board of Directors. I wrote this book with their blessing. Special thanks to Beth McKee who led the Board while I was writing this book. Others on the Center's board include Matthew Myer Boulton, Lant Davis, Richard Hamm, Michael Jinkins, and Katie Patterson,

Every time I talk with Craig Dykstra I learn important things about religion and about life. I met him as my teacher. He is still my teacher and friend.

I've had excellent pastors in my life. Two who keep me focused on essential things are William Enright and Richard Baker.

I've served two congregations as pastor: Bethlehem Presbyterian Church in Logansport, Indiana, and Westminster Presbyterian Church in Xenia, Ohio. I learned more from these blessed communities than I could ever return in kind.

This book would not exist without Floyd "Buzz" Reed. He makes sacrifices every day for others. Buzz co-led classes on this material. Everything he read, he made better. James Rafferty is an advisor I wish more people could learn from. He holds uncommon insight into human beings and human community. Barry Kibel's wisdom is matched by his unique, effective ways of creating learning journeys for organizations and individuals.

Thanks to Juliana Wilhelm and the Townsend Leadership Group.

The graphics were ably prepared by David Stahl of Stahl Strategic Design.

Special thanks to Chris Fischer, Carli Hansen, and Sarah Stanton with Rowman & Littlefield. I am grateful for their patience and expertise. They know how to move a book, with excellence and clarity, through the production process. I am appreciative of the copyediting work contributed by Naomi Mindlin and the proofreading work contributed by Kimberly Giambattisto.

Any mistakes, lapses in clarity, unhelpful comments, and just plain errors are my responsibility and my responsibility alone. Anything helpful in this book is because I learned from the people named above.

I'm married to Gretchen. We have three sons and a daughter-in-law: Jacob and Katelyn, Ian, and Eli. My family—they are all amazing.

Introduction

The Congregation as a Learning Community

I wrote this book because I want to help your congregation learn to accomplish important things. This book isn't just about your congregation doing something new. It is about your congregation *learning* to do something new. The premise of the book is that your congregation learns as it accomplishes new things and thus builds capacity to take on new challenges.

Not only does your congregation learn as it accomplishes new things, but your congregation also learns in a discernible way. Congregations that effectively implement new endeavors travel a journey—what I call a "learning journey"—with specific passages along the way. This book is about those passages that include defining your challenge, exploration of the issue, disappointment, discovery, taking on and letting go, validation, and then, inevitably, another challenge. As your congregation travels this journey it inhabits what it means to be a learning community. Yes, your congregation is a learning organization—one that facilitates the deeper knowledge of clergy and laity so as to effectively address ever more complex endeavors.

Congregations face many kinds of tests. Some are mundane. The roof leaks. The parking lot needs repaving. The microphones don't work well. Some tests are transcendent. How should lives be honored? What is God calling the congregation to do and be? How can generosity be taught? Just as you and I as individuals face situations for which we are not prepared—the death of a parent, a decision about health care—congregational leaders face challenges that are just beyond the grasp of their abilities. This book addresses the just-beyond-the-grasp challenges in the context of a learning journey.

I do not consider myself primarily an author. I am not a researcher, although the findings in this book are well documented. I have been a pastor of small and medium-sized churches so the book is in some ways founded on firsthand experience. I am not a consultant to congregations, at least not in a typical way. Most of this book is derived from my experience leading the Indianapolis Center for Congregations. The Center is a nonprofit funded by the Lilly Endowment. The Center has a twofold mission: to strengthen congregations by helping them find and use resources to address their challenges and opportunities, and then to share what it is learning with a national audience. During my fourteen years at the Center, I have worked with more than 1,100 congregations and the Center in total has worked with more than 4,000 congregations.

Thus my colleagues and I have a unique perspective. We have discovered that congregational strength is directly linked to a congregation's ability to learn. Furthermore, the learning journey is apparent in congregations that effectively address their challenges and opportunities. I did not invent the process. I observed it. The process can be mapped. The process is part of the natural dynamics of human community. By being aware of what happens naturally, you can be a more creative agent in your congregation's efforts to accomplish remarkable things.

I want you to know that the stories and illustrations in this book come from my experience working with congregations. I intentionally write from an appreciative point of view. In many instances, in order to maintain anonymity for the subjects, I have omitted names, places, and other details of many of the examples. In some cases, I have created composites in order to preserve anonymity. In every instance I seek to convey the true learning that came from the original context and details. Where I name a clergyperson or staff person, I have received permission to do so.

As for you, the reader, note that I address you directly as "you." I do this to signal that I intend the book's content to be a conversation, imagined at least, if not real. I believe the contents of the book can be helpful to clergy and laity alike.

I pray that your congregation will more effectively achieve what it seeks to do for the building up of the congregation and for the sake of God's world.

USING THIS BOOK

This book will provide you access to practical steps you can take immediately to move new ideas or long-term challenges along in your congregation. You will learn sound ways for your congregation to function as a learning community. You can read the book through or pause to practice one skill (for example, the art of asking open-ended questions). The book is suitable for a book study group. There are many examples that a group can learn from in order to increase readiness to take on a challenge or opportunity. The outcome of engaging this book is simple: *Your congregation will be able to achieve what it sets out to do.*

WHAT THIS BOOK IS ABOUT

There is a discernible learning journey that takes place in congregations that accomplish worthwhile projects. The learning experience exists even if you are not conscious of it. However, if you can see and identify the learning, then you will be able to more purposefully achieve those things that your congregation is drawn to do. Making the learning journey more explicit can save wear and tear on you and those who are leaders in your congregation. You will be able to anticipate earlier what you need to do, thus lowering frustration. In the chapters that follow you will learn about each of the steps along the way of the journey. You will learn about actions or behaviors that will help your congregation to do new things well.

Undertaking a strategic learning journey isn't necessary or even helpful for many congregational tasks. For example, if your congregation has become quite capable of hosting a feeding ministry, you don't need to go through extensive steps to continue this work. Or maybe you want to establish a new accounting procedure and there is already someone in your congregation who knows how to do this. It would be a waste of time to go through an entire learning experience to set up a new financial system that someone already knows how to implement.

Instead, the process of learning is most applicable when you want to accomplish something that requires you to realize new behaviors. This organizational learning is most useful when the demands that you face are new, confusing, and create discomfort. Don't waste your time digging into a learning journey for something you have mastered. Do pay attention to these dynamics when the task at hand extends beyond your congregation's current capacity. (Ronald Heifetz describes this as discerning the difference between a technical and an adaptive challenge.[1])

Here's an example. An Indiana congregation wants to start a new summer program for youth who live nearby. The subject of the program will be music. The reason for the program is that many neighborhood children are left on their own during the summer without direction or meaningful activities. The pastor and other leaders want the church to be a place where children receive the attention they deserve, participating in an activity that brings joy.

When considering the program, one leader in the church says, "Well, this is certainly something we've never done before." The idea of a summer program is new. At the first team meeting, the group spends an hour debating what the initial step should be. The task is confusing. After that first meeting, e-mails go back and forth with team members expressing concern about whether or not the program will be successful. One person writes, "Right now, I'm anxious. We're clueless." People are experiencing discomfort.

This congregation will benefit from leaders becoming more aware of the pattern of learning that exists and is available to most congregations. This pattern includes a journey from identifying the challenge accurately, to moments of discovery, to validation of the learning that has occurred. The journey of organizational learning applies best to congregations that are designing and implementing activities, tactics, and programs that are beyond their current capacity. The learning dynamics are not just theoretical. They are practical and actionable.

THE METHOD

Learning is the achievement of new abilities as representations of new thinking, effective behaviors, and the positive regulation of emotions. Of course, an organization like a congregation does not itself learn; actually, it is individuals in the organization who learn together in order to accomplish something new. When this happens it is as if the congregation has learned.

Peter Senge is the author of a classic book on learning organizations. In his book *The Fifth Discipline* he writes,

> Learning organizations are possible because not only is it our nature to learn but we love to learn. Most of us at one time or another have been part of a great team, a group of people who functioned together in an extraordinary way—who trusted one another, who complemented one another's strengths and compensated for one another's limitation, who had common goals that were larger than individual goals, and who produced extraordinary results. I have met many people who have experienced this sort of profound teamwork—in sports, or in the performing arts, or in business. Many say that they have spent much of their life looking for that experience again. What they experienced was a learning organization. [2]

*A **learning congregation** facilitates the development of new abilities of its clergy and laity so as to continuously improve its capacity to address ever-increasing demands for the sake of religious claims and commitments.* The word *ability* denotes the reality that clergy and laity will learn new skills. Proficiency will increase. The reality that both *clergy and laity* are involved reveals that congregational learning involves people beyond the professional class of clergy serving formal roles. The need to *continuously improve* is a reality. Congregational life always presents demands beyond one's current talent. One thing that distinguishes congregations from other learning communities is that communities of faith ultimately seek to learn *for the sake of religious claims and commitments*. The dividing line between the secular and the religious (if such a division makes sense any more—and it may not) is not so clear. Yet, congregations are ultimately religious communities. Congregational learning is ultimately for the sake of transcendent meaning.

This methodology is a developmental learning approach. To distinguish it from other valid approaches, it is not a strictly a theological method, a systems approach, or a therapeutic-based approach. The approach is not about weaknesses, threats, or diagnosing failure. The model is centered on learning. Therefore, it includes aspects of many models including the ones noted above. The experience of congregational learning encompasses theology, systems thinking, behaviors, feelings, and ultimately the implementation of new ideas.

What does it mean to apply a developmental learning approach to your congregation? Think of developmental learning in terms of an individual. Throughout an individual's life there is opportunity to acquire new skills. We know that, based on brain development, motor skills, environment, genetics, emotional regulation, and so forth, individuals are able to learn certain life tasks at certain points along the life cycle. For many, acquisition of language is developed at an early age. Working on complex mathematic problems like knot theory is a capacity that very few have and for those very few it typically develops in their early twenties. Learning forgiveness or learning to love an enemy are lifelong developmental tasks that have to do with character development. The point is that all our learning is developmental. As individuals we learn new abilities as we grow. It is a process with fits and starts. Such learning is influenced by a number of factors. There are genetic factors as well as contextual factors. Emotions as well as external demands are factors. A key element is matching the capacity for growth with the demands of the task. As the poet Robert Lowell writes to our country concerning abolishing slavery, "New occasions teach new duties."[3]

Now, your congregation learns developmentally, too. Your capacity to do new things is related to your readiness as well as the difficulty of the task. Reading through 1 Corinthians, I was struck by the way the apostle Paul writes from a developmental framework (though would he even call it that?). One could say that 1 Corinthians is a letter to an early church community learning new duties based on new situations. The letter addresses the demands of faith within their metropolitan setting. Paul addresses issues that are diverse. He addresses complicated issues of the day including sexual morality; the role of women in the church; eating practices, including the meal representing Christ's death and resurrection; spiritual gifts, and much more. He speaks developmentally when he states, "I fed you with milk, not solid food, for you were not ready for solid food" (1 Cor. 3:2). The distinctive and well-known love passage from 1 Corinthians 13:11–12 uses developmental language: "When I was a child, I spoke like a child, I thought like a child, I reasoned like a child; when I became an adult, I put an end to childish ways. For now we see in a mirror, dimly, but then we will see face to face. Now I know only in part; then I will know fully, even as I have been fully known."

So to say this approach uses a developmental learning model is to simply (or not so simply) state that your congregation has the potential to take on new activities in concert with *learning* new ways of thinking, feeling, and acting. Such learning does not happen all at once. It happens over time, incrementally, yet with forward momentum.

LEARNING RELATIONSHIPS

In addition to the community in Corinth, congregations have historically been seen as places of learning. The early church was a place for study and teaching (as were synagogues). In some religious traditions, congregational leaders are called teachers. This is true is some Protestant traditions like the Presbyterian tradition where the pastor is called a "teaching elder." This is also true in the Jewish tradition where the congregational spiritual leader is called "rabbi." After all, the word "rabbi" denotes a teacher. Rabbi Jonathan Sacks reflects on learning, leaders, and religious community this way: "If a leader seeks to make lasting change, he or she must follow in the footsteps of Moses and become an educator. The leader-as-teacher, using influence not power, spiritual and intellectual authority rather than coercive force, was one of the greatest contributions Judaism ever made to the moral horizons of humankind."[4]

Unlike many other organizations, learning relationships in congregations occur beyond formal roles. Learning takes place *between* the primary beneficiaries of services as well as decision makers. The relationships in which learning takes place in congregations are more egalitarian than some other cultural settings (for example, a hierarchical corporation). This sometimes awkward alignment of roles is made less awkward not through a system analysis or a SWOT (strengths, weaknesses, opportunities, threats) analysis, but through experiences of learning to do new things together. Learning best takes place in a community of authentic, healthy affection for one another. What better way to create such a sense of community than a nurturing a disposition toward learning.

I want to encourage you to think of the challenges your congregation faces in terms of what you are learning and what you still need to learn. This is a developmental learning perspective.

Consider these examples. A large nondenominational congregation moves from being a once-a-week gathering of two thousand members to providing opportunities of faith formation in small groups of twelve meeting every other week.

A small rural United Methodist Church goes from being a congregation where the vocation of farming was what members did during the week to integrating this positive reality with also being a rural community center focusing on the needs of farm families.

A suburban Lutheran congregation changes its youth program from being Sunday evening pizza gatherings to focusing on an annual mission theme.

These developments all occurred because the respective congregations learned new behaviors. Each congregation went on a journey, if you will, where it began at one place and ended in another, not just with a new program, but with a new view of itself, new ways of thinking, and new capacity. This is what happens when a congregation views its challenges through the frame of being a learning community.

Why do some congregations struggle while others thrive? Why do some congregations falter while others face their challenges with the sturdiness of Moses in the wilderness? The demands on congregational life are much different than even a decade ago. I contend that the primary factor in the decline of the congregation (that is occurring in some, but not all settings) is best viewed through the frame of capacity in relationship to demands, not other various sociological reasons. In other words, there is nothing inherently wrong with your congregation. Rather unsuspectingly, the pressures placed upon your faith community have outpaced the capacity of your worshiping community. This is a developmental diagnosis based on observing human response to the contemporary demands of life. This is true whether the demand is related to interpreting the reality of grace or choosing which asphalt company is the best to resurface the parking lot. This is true in almost all spheres of contemporary life, not just congregations. Think of the changes in the last decade in dealing with health insurance companies. Or think of what it is like for an eighteen year old to adjust to his or her first semester at college. Greater demands, when experienced in congregational life, create a need for clergy and laity to learn effective ways of addressing challenges so that they maintain agency over their problems rather than the problems having a hold on them (applying a phrase used by Robert Kegan and Lisa Lahey).[5] In congregations, as in other arenas of life, a problem can have a hold on you, or through the process of learning you can discover how to take hold of that challenge.

A lay leader helped her Methodist congregation take hold of a challenge. She (and others) wanted to build a prayer wall in the gathering space. The desire was for a place where prayers could be written on paper and then inserted into spaces in the wall as an offering to God. With the council's approval, she gathered a team that spent two months studying prayer practices, as well as the history of Jerusalem's Western Wall. The team's consultation with an architect was framed as a learning experience. Soon, a stone wall was constructed, placed, and blessed in the gathering space. Now, new prayers are added daily. People hold in their hands the prayers they have written. Then, they carefully insert the pieces of paper with their petitions written on them between the stones. In addition to the Lord's Prayer, communal prayers, silent prayer, and other forms of prayer, worshipers have learned a new way to pray. "We started with the need to deepen our prayer life; we moved to learning and then to action," the lay leader explains.

The congregations that are thriving, those that are doing beautiful and powerful things in relationship to their religious claims and commitments, are those that learn in ways that extend their capacity to take hold of challenges rather than let the challenges control them.[6] These congregations travel a developmental learning journey. They learn how to address the demands that, for the moment, are just beyond their grasp. Soon the demands will be in their hands, being shaped and formed for the life God has given them.

To what degree will you become more conscious of positive learning dynamics to reach the goals that are most important to you? Regardless of the issue, regardless of what resource or method you use, gaining capacity to effectively reach your congregational goal is an educational endeavor. There is no diploma at the end, yet there is the intrinsic satisfaction that you are using your heart, mind, and soul for God's purposes.

The learning journey will help you and your congregation do new things consistent with that which matters most to your faith community. The demands placed on congregations are many. Yet, the possibilities are like the feeling one gets when looking at a beautiful landscape for the first time. It is feeling as if you are entering into a great, wide-open space; heaven and earth are meeting; and the difficult-yet-important is suddenly possible.

It is time to begin the journey.

Chapter One

The Journey

Patterns and Behaviors

What do you do when your congregation chooses to do something new? Perhaps your congregation wants to start a homeless ministry. Maybe your congregation is working on renovation of the building and it has been more than a decade since a significant building project. Perhaps you and your colleagues want to encourage faith formation in a different way. The new thing could be addressing a long-term issue that the congregation has avoided. No one needs help in creating a list of new demands on a congregation. Each can seem like starting a deep-space mission. Your congregation is often in a situation where it is expected to think and behave in ways that it has not yet learned with knowledge it does not yet hold.

If the tasks are unfamiliar or if the content and the process are not clear, then your congregation will need to learn new behaviors in order to achieve your goals.

What is learning? Learning is durable change in behavior. It almost always emanates from experience. You read something (reading is an experience). You now think differently. Or you are at a workshop. The teacher describes a fresh way of doing a task. You go back home. You try something unique. You reflect on your experience. Repeat. Now, you have learned. The change endures.

Of course, for a congregation to learn new behavior, individuals who are part of that congregation need to learn. It is possible to assert that organizations learn. When organizational learning takes place it is because individuals engaged with one another are taking on new ways of thinking. The individuals experience durable behavioral change as part of the organization.

Accomplishing new things requires organizational learning. Think back on a time when your congregation accomplished something new. You might say that your congregation started a new program. If it is indeed a new program, then it is more accurate to say your congregation *learned* to start a new program. Did your congregation reorganize its committee structure? It is more precise to say that your congregation *learned* a new way of decision making.

Learning is a comprehensive frame that encompasses many approaches to building congregational capacity. For example, some frames emphasize leadership. Some highlight a specific theological perspective. Some paradigms focus on external assessments, such as understanding a local community or a particular generation of people. Some approaches involve naming and claiming strengths. Your congregation may have used these approaches to acquire new knowledge. You then turned that knowledge into new behaviors.

One congregation started their path to achieve something new because of babies. The conversation began in the basement of the church. A woman sitting in a rocking chair was with three others. She remarked, "I used to rock all my babies. Every night we fell asleep together." Her friend said, "I just read that our town has babies that need rocking."

This conversation led to more. Soon the two women were talking with their pastor about starting a rocking chair ministry for babies at the county daycare for infants and toddlers. A brief announcement in worship a month later yielded nine volunteers. When the church volunteers showed up at the daycare to sign up, they were met with a friendly but firm "no." It turns out that you can't just show up and be handed a baby. You have to be trained. Volunteers have to participate in a six-week course in proper and tender care of infants. The school needs to run background checks. The director has to meet with the pastor. For this congregation to begin a new program, individuals were going to have to learn new ways of doing something as natural as holding a baby.

That's exactly what happened next. This group of nine women and men began a journey to learn how to do ministry at a public daycare. They reported back to the church board. They registered for the training class. The congregation hosted three civic conversations that covered public health issues and psychological dynamics like attachment theory. During Lent, the pastor preached on baptism and public ministry. The congregation learned new behaviors related to working with a nonprofit. As a community of faith, individuals learned the new behavior of rocking babies to sleep, not at home in the nursery, but in a public setting for the common good.

EDUCATION VERSUS TRAINING

Congregations that learn new behaviors go on a discernible learning journey. An identifiable model can be observed in congregations that learn to do new things well. This book will take you through this model, or what I'm calling a "journey." Yet, before we start such an expedition I want to note that not all endeavors in the congregation need to be conceived as a learning journey. Not all endeavors in the congregation require acquisition of new knowledge or different behaviors.

Educator Robert Kegan notes the difference between education and training.[1] Training is an informational stance. It leaves your view of the world essentially the same. Education is different. It changes the essential nature of who you are. The word *education* is built out of the Latin verb that means "to lead." Education leads you out from one construct of life to another. Education is what leads to transformation.

Some congregational challenges require information. If you want to begin a Facebook page for your congregation, there are people who can show you how to do it. You are not going to have to change something essential about yourself in order to accomplish this. You can be trained. If you want to make Wi-Fi more readily available in your building, there are people who can show you how to do it. There are people who can do this for you. You are not going to change something essential about your congregation in order to achieve this.

However, if your congregation wants to extend itself to address a challenge that is currently just beyond its capacity to handle, then education is needed. Typically, such challenges involve those things that matter deeply to the congregation. Such challenges of consequence require growth in you and in those with whom you experience life together in your faith community. You and I can be trained to create a budget but we need to be educated to be generous. You and I can be trained to interpret scripture, but we need to be educated to practice our faith. We can be trained to learn a second language but we need to be educated to carry out an effective program teaching others a second language. Our congregations can be the place where we not only gain information about God (just who is God anyway?), but also fall in love with God's creation.

Defining the task of a new endeavor in your congregation as a "learning journey" reinforces the reality that life is a school from which none of us graduate. What better testimony to the importance of congregational life than for congregational life to be a place for lifelong learning.

A congregation wanting to immerse itself in silent prayer will participate in active learning; members will learn by doing. A congregation seeking to start a new worship site across town may want to consult with other congregations who have done something similar. Raising funds through a capital campaign could be framed in terms of the amount needed to be pledged. Or it could be constructed as a learning challenge—an opportunity to absorb new values about faith and money. All these endeavors are educational. For congregations, such endeavors involve growth through experience. This is what I mean by a "learning journey."

PASSAGES THROUGH THE LEARNING JOURNEY

After observing congregations learning about many different challenges, I have witnessed a pattern in congregations that accomplished what they set out to do. This pattern includes eight discernible experiences that are part of the learning journey. If we were to examine thirty congregations and their efforts to take on new activities, we would not encounter all eight in each case. However, taken together we would see many of these aspects of the journey throughout the stories.

The learning journey is not always straight and true. There are starts and stops along the way. Learning in community consists of roundabouts and chicanes. However, it is instructive to view the model in a linear fashion, at least as you acquaint yourself with the process. This helps to make the implicit more explicit. As you become more familiar with how your congregation learns, you will see there is more than one route to new capacity. For now, though, let's look at the learning journey in an ideal state in order to become familiar with what your congregation might encounter.

A congregation in the Midwest takes to heart Psalm 46:10, "Be still and know that I am God!" The clergy leader asks the board to designate November the month of silent prayer. The board, not quite sure what they are endorsing, trust the pastor and agree to such a designation.

Now, the pastor plans a Sunday evening class on the practice of silent prayer. He purchases copies of *Centering Prayer and Inner Awakening* by Cynthia Bourgeault for the participants to read.[2] As he walks through the door prepared for the first gathering, a person already sitting in the room asks, "Now, exactly why are doing this?" It is important to know why you are taking on a new endeavor.

The first part of the learning journey for the congregation is *defining the challenge*. The congregation seeks to answer the question, "Why are we doing this?" Congregations that accomplish goals are clear about the challenge or opportunity they are undertaking. What needs to be learned, what need to be accomplished, is more attainable when congregational leaders leave little doubt about the task at hand and how the task fits into an overall purpose.

The second phase of a healthy learning journey is *exploration*. This is when a congregation considers how to respond to the challenge. This involves scanning the contours of the challenge. It is like looking out on a new landscape and getting acquainted with the scene—the way the sun rises, the shadows of the trees, the way the clouds move at the horizon. This phase involves searching for possibilities, using resources to learn more, and getting the right number of people (and the right people) involved.

During the exploration passage of the journey, a congregation seeking to start a worship service at another site conducts a demographic assessment of the new neighborhood. The board consults with two congregations in other towns that had started satellite sites. The pastor shares his vision with more people as the plan becomes more clear. Members of the worship team read a book on the arts and liturgy. The exploration phase is a time when congregational leaders acquire information that they hope in God's good time will lead to a moment of discovery. Patience and focus are necessary virtues during exploration.

As congregational leaders tell stories about achieving new things, it is common to hear of *disappointment*. A rural congregation seeks to build a new structure that is to serve as an education center on Sundays and a community meeting place during the week. Their original building, constructed in 1856, has room for only one Sunday School class. During the week, there is no place for the local service club to meet. To meet the challenge of providing more space for religious education and community gatherings, an architect creates conceptual drawings. Based on the drawings, the architect estimates the project cost would be $1.1 million. The capital campaign consultant reports that the congregation, based on current data, could count on raising $500,000. When the pastor is presented this information he says, "I feel like someone just closed the door to my dream." Learning journeys often require you to respond to the inevitability of obstacles. Sometimes an obstacle is the end of the journey. At other times, an obstacle is God's direction in disguise.

Often coming to terms with disappointment and effective exploration leads to *discovery*. This is a flash of clarity. It is an instance of decision. Sometimes it is described as an aha moment. Most of us have heard the cliché description of how a teacher can see the light bulb turn on in the student's mind at the moment of recognition. This can also happen for congregational leaders. The light-bulb moment is indeed a revelation like a burning bush, a mountaintop transfiguration, an epiphany along an Emmaus road. It may seem that the discovery has come out of nowhere. In retrospect it becomes apparent that key discoveries are a result of both grace and hard work.[3]

A discovery, a sense of clear direction, results in an evolutionary state of *letting go and taking on*. For example, the congregation seeking to build the new education and community center decides that in order to live within financial means, they will let go of some items designed on paper by the architect. Simultaneously, the planning team decides that they need to pay more attention to finances. The building team sets a challenge goal of $850,000. The team assigns trusted members to plan precisely all parts of the project having to do with fund-raising. Before, they had said simply, "God will provide." Now, they are functioning as if God was challenging them to deliver on the finances. Letting go and taking on in some ways might be seen as strategic operational moves. They are. But they are more than that, too. Letting go and taking on are spiritual experiences that require a new mindset, a change in understanding, a leap of faith based on an evocative discovery.

Congregations that effectively learn to meet their challenges ultimately experience *validation* of their endeavors. During the validation phase the congregation confirms that the effort was worthwhile, that something of importance was learned, and that the congregation would do it all over again if needed. Validation is often expressed in a story—a story that represents a change in attitude or behavior. Sometimes validation is experienced through results—more people attending, more funds raised, more events hosted. Sometimes validation is indicated by sensing a "happy hum" in the congregation.

Of course, when a congregation learns to address a challenge well, there is always going to be the eighth passage to a new challenge. When interviewing congregations that have taken on something new, they often have an answer to the question, "So, what's next?" In other words, there is always a *new challenge*.

The journey from the first passage of defining a challenge to the presentation of another new challenge describes the pattern of a congregational learning journey. It is helpful to identify these phases because they normalize otherwise difficult transitions that congregations experience when taking on new challenges.

Making the learning journey an explicit part of your congregation's experience lowers frustration. Viewing the experience as learning normalizes the experience. Making the learning journey explicit is a way for you as a congregational leader to maintain initiative in relationship to the challenge. You aren't a passive observer. You are an active learner.

Plus, an explicit uncovering of the sometimes subtle learning journey creates a safer landscape for risk. It is like having a GPS map to your destination on your phone when you get into the car. Having more leaders in your congregation understand what is going on (and what to expect) provides immunization against the inescapable tough days that are part of doing anything worthwhile.

A COMPARISON MODEL

After observing the learning journey in so many congregations I wondered if there were other conceptual frameworks regarding organizational learning. Peter Senge describes core disciplines. These disciplines include personal mastery, mental models, shared vision, and team learning (see his book *The Fifth Discipline*).[4] These are activities. They do not constitute a narrative journey.

Various models of strategic planning describe what might be called a path for the process of planning. But a path for planning is not necessarily the same as learning.

After more consideration I found similarities between the congregational learning journey and models of individual growth. For example, Joseph Campbell writes about the hero's journey.[5] Such a journey includes the call to adventure, the refusal of the call, an intervention, and so forth. It is based on mythic undercurrents. It is found in many ancient narratives.

I found another contemporary framework for individual development. I wasn't looking for it. It was a discovery. I was sitting in my office at home. I was looking through books, sifting through ones perhaps ready to find a new home at a local used bookstore. There it was: *The Transforming Moment* by James Loder.[6] He was a beloved Princeton Theological Seminary professor. In *The Transforming Moment* and other books, Loder describes a five-stage passage that people experience when they move through transformation.[7] The five passages include conflict, search for resolution, imagination, release

Figure 1.1.   Learning Journey. The learning journey represents what congregations experience when they learn to do something new. Although the order may differ from what is depicted, almost all of the experiences naturally occur when a congregation effectively develops a new program or initiative.

of energy, and verification. Loder proposes, through listening to people's life stories, that these elements occur when one goes through life-changing experiences.

Now, Loder's passage is based on observing individuals, while the congregational learning journey is based on observing faith communities. However, when I became acquainted with Loder's observations I noticed similarities. Loder asserts that the logic of individual transformation begins with conflict—experiences of discontinuity. Similarly, the challenge that a congregation experiences is characterized by unease if not conflict. The individual search for resolution is similar to the learning congregation's exploration. The release of energy is parallel to the revelation aspects of discovery. Loder's verification is in some way parallel to the way congregations naturally validate what they have learned.

The comparison I made between the Loder work and the learning journey means to me that this isn't something I invented; rather, it is something I observed. The reality that similar observations are being made in other fields signifies that the movement of learning identified in congregations is part of how humans work. It represents not only a conceptual framework, but also something real in creation that has existed for some time, existing just below the surface of our awareness.

FUNDAMENTAL BEHAVIORS FOR THE JOURNEY

In addition to identifying an underlying journey, I have observed several fundamental behaviors that help move the congregation along the learning experience.

The central and most important behavior is *the congregation's ability to learn from an outside resource plus its own creativity*. This is the process of juxtaposing what you learn from a helper with your own ingenuity. Your congregation has the best chance of flourishing when an outside resource is used in concert with the congregation's own assets and creativity in order to address a challenge. The outside resource might be another congregation that has addressed a similar challenge, or it might be a book about the task at hand. The resource might be a website, or a consultant—any resource that encourages you to think precisely and to move others from private opinions to a more comprehensive appraisal of the situation. Your creativity is needed because almost every resource needs to be adapted to your situation. This adaptation involves taking the principles of a resource and applying that learning to your context. The adaptation is needed because what are called "best practices" are not always transferable to a variety of contexts. The principles of an approach may be helpful, but the specific actions are typically not portable. Hence, the need for your creativity.

Congregations that succeed at new efforts have leaders skilled at *the art of conversation*. If members of the faith community have the experience of being truly heard, they are more likely to focus on possibilities and solutions rather than getting caught on problems. Often a precursor to listening is asking "open-ended" questions, not "leading" questions. The art of conversation also includes proper timing of certain messages, having mantras to lean on when things get complicated, and additional subtle communication cues, such as making sure that affirmations outnumber criticisms.

Many important congregational issues do not require a sense of urgency. Congregations make their best decisions when they align *measured timing* to the tasks at hand. Thus understanding how an appropriate pace is at work in your journey helps you make wise decisions. Sometimes you will need to slow down the process. The very act of learning from an outside resource slows down decision-making processes and subsequently contributes to clear thinking among congregational leaders.

What does slowing down look like? It is as much a way of thinking about strategy as it is a literal timeline. The slowing down may take many forms. It might be as subtle as slowing the pace of a particular conversation so that questions can be asked and answers can be explored. Decelerating your congregation's strategic thinking is a way to counter the inevitable rush to judgment that many groups experience while making decisions. Such haste is rarely due to the absolute necessity of a quick decision.

Congregations learn well when they attend to *rites of passage*. When new learning is taking place it is important for congregations to pay attention to tender and powerful moments of existence: birth, graduation, marriage, divorce, illness, recovery, and death. Attention to rites of passage, which are distillations of developmental experiences, confirms a culture of learning for a congregation. Nothing teaches like life.

Congregations that learn well have the ability to think clearly about God and then act accordingly. I call this the capacity for *religious coherence*. A congregation that is clear and consistent about how it understands God and applies this understanding to its daily life is more able to deal effectively with challenges and opportunities. There is a correlation between the ability of leaders to think and speak lucidly about religious matters and congregational capacity.

Congregations that accomplish what they set out to do have leaders who are lifelong learners. Such congregations have clergy and lay leaders for whom an essential component of leading is learning and helping others to learn. Leadership and learning go together. They are not separate endeavors. In such congregations, *clergy and laity learn side by side*. Certainly there are differences between roles and functions, but generally clergy and laity experience each other as trusted partners on the same journey. Clergy have their own specialized knowledge that is invaluable to the congregation. Yet, clergy's special knowledge is most valuable when combined with the knowledge of able members of the congregation. Individual congregants have their own specialized knowledge that is beneficial for the religious community. Shared learning between clergy and laity builds respect and a strong commitment to common goals, thus increasing the chance that ideas will come to fruition.

The behaviors described will serve you well through different passages of your congregation's learning journey.

THREE REALMS OF LEARNING

It doesn't matter if the challenge has to do with a mission trip or with a master design of the facility; the learning journey is remarkably similar. There are three realms of learning in a congregation: the religious realm, the life-practice realm, and the organizational realm. Regardless of the realm in which the learning resides, the journey elements are present.

The religious realm includes challenges that overtly address matters of faith, such as learning from scripture, practicing prayer, and enhancing worship.

The life-practice realm includes ways congregations formally and informally help congregants improve their practice of day-to-day activities such as managing household finances, balancing work and family, preparing for marriage, and experiencing rites of passage.

The organizational realm includes learning about managing congregational operations, such as staff supervision, building upkeep, creating budgets, running meetings, and discerning strategic plans.

It helps to know the realm in which the challenge you are addressing primarily resides. The risk is that the congregation will focus its attention on the realm in which it is most proficient. Some congregations have fine structures and processes in place for operations. When this is true, you will find your congregation paying more attention to details of organization. Such focus will ultimately be at the detriment of attention paid to religious or life-practice learning.

Powerful learning takes place when the three realms intersect. In vital congregations there is a balance and intersection of the attention paid to these three realms. A rural congregation is seeking to merge with another. At first most of the conversation has to do with finances, pastoral leadership, and answering questions having to do with the two buildings. The leaders concentrate on the organizational realm of their life together because that is where most of their attention has gone the last five years. However, there are members of each congregation longing for support and education about pressing life subjects: end-of-life decisions, facing death, and taking care of aging parents. When the respective boards of the two congregations start

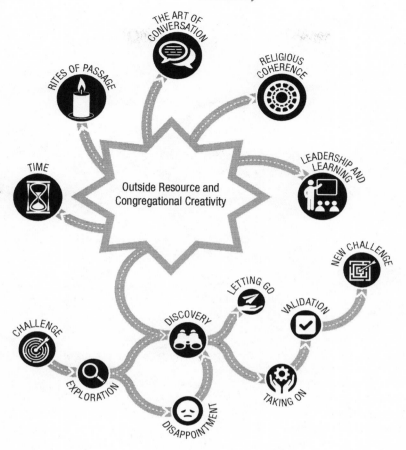

Figure 1.2. Behaviors and the Journey. Several behaviors support the progress of a learning journey. The primary action is using an outside resource alongside the congregation's creativity. All the behaviors create positive conditions within the congregation for learning to take place.

hosting community gatherings around these life-practice subjects, the leaders begin simultaneously to make progress on the organizational challenges.

WHY BOTHER? MAKING THE IMPLICIT MORE EXPLICIT

Why bother with understanding the learning patterns and the fundamental behaviors along the way, let alone making sense of what resource fits what challenge? There are plenty of other matters of importance. In any congrega-

Religious Learning

Organizational Learning

Life Practice Learning

Figure 1.3.   Three Realms. At any given time in a congregation, learning is taking place in one or more of these three realms. The most powerful learning occurs when some aspect of each of these realms is being addressed in the same initiative, project, or program.

tion, no matter the size, there are urgent tasks that need attention. There isn't time or motivation to see each task as a learning opportunity.

However, congregations exist for the very reason of making the implicit more explicit. Congregations carry outlines of God just waiting to be represented more fully. Congregations hold divine associations on the edge of more robust depiction. The presence of the divine is often implied rather than plainly expressed. When Moses came across the burning bush, the epiphany of God's presence revealed something that before had not been plainly expressed. An implicit desire for God became explicit in that fiery rendering.

As a leader, being more aware of your congregation's learning journeys will help you more directly express what is unfolding in your faith community.

The explication of the journey will increase satisfaction with congregational life. It will minimize risk and increase achievement. The learning journeys that your congregation take are expeditions into revelation. Along the way that which was only known in part becomes more fully known. Revelation resulting in deeper knowledge occurs when a congregation functions as a place for lifelong learning that is developmental. Congregations can be one of the primary communities that foster the continuing growth of what it means to be a human being in one's own inner life, in relationships, and in community engagement.

A congregation's learning journey not only changes something important about the congregation; it can change a person's life, too. At first it seemed impossible. The church wanted to raise two million dollars to add to the fellowship hall. For seven years—and three pastors—the idea was stuck. Why do we need a new fellowship hall? At one meeting someone said (simply and finally), "Well, if we ever are going to truly feed strangers rather than just hand out food, we need a larger fellowship hall." The result of this long-awaited clarity was that in six months they raised 1.7 million dollars. A year and a half later the fellowship hall was complete. Soon after came the first weekday dinner open to the community. On that Tuesday evening, seventy-seven (to be exact) people ate spaghetti and meatballs in the newly renovated fellowship hall. For most of the time, a woman, let's call her Helen—a school teacher who serves on the board—sat in the corner with another woman. The pastor was aware of this. He knew Helen but he didn't know who the other woman was. He knew better than to interrupt. He watched. Both women were crying. Then, they were both smiling.

The next day Helen stopped by the church to drop off a document for the board meeting. She asked if the pastor was available. She waited in the hallway. It appeared that she wasn't sure whether to sit down or walk out. Something was stirring. (We won't know the full story.) When the pastor walked up he said, "Hey, what's going on?" Helen said, "I just want you to know that God changed my life last night."

Of course, God changes lives every day. A quiet conversation between two strangers can be a sign of God at work. We change every day. We affect others all the time. What contributes to such change, and is *change* even the best word to use?

THEORY OF DEVELOPMENT

Congregations espouse beautiful messages about what is most important in life. They advance rich traditions concerning grace, salvation, charity, love for neighbor and self, generosity, devotion, and many more life-giving assertions. However, congregations are also frustrating communities. Rarely do other human assemblies frustratingly fail so comprehensively to live up to their proclamations. Congregations paradoxically allow and promote behaviors we would never allow in our families, or only allow in our families. When this happens, a chasm grows between the beautiful messages that congregations proclaim and what they practice. Congregations become poorly functioning institutions rather than places that promote human beings living into the full stature of their potential.

Think of what can be accomplished for the sake of the world if congregations increase their capacity for being creative, innovative, flexible, and challenging. It can be done without compromising religious claims and commitments. Indeed, such an approach raises the stakes of taking such religious claims and commitments more seriously and with greater passion.

Whether or not it is explicit, your congregation functions with certain assumptions about development. Your congregation operates with a repertoire of values that shapes its ability to learn. Your congregation employs these values through a variety of behaviors. Some of these behaviors make learning more possible. Some of these behaviors are conscious blockades. Some are unconscious obstructions. Your congregation functions with a theory of development whether or not you are conscious of it.

There are all kinds of theories related to development, learning, change, growth, and so forth. Some are tested and validated. Some are hypothetical. When Frank's wife says, "He won't stop smoking until he's ready," she's expressing, probably unknowingly, a theory of development. Your congregation's implicit theory of development may be rooted in a theological view of humanity focusing on the fall of creation. Or perhaps it is informed by who holds power in your faith community. Maybe your congregation's experience of development is shaped by Jesus Christ's death and resurrection—that is, learning happens through God's initiative and follows a pattern of loss and new life.

What is happening in vibrant congregations is development, not change. The word *change* is problematic. The *result* may be some kind of change, yet congregations that effectively do new things don't necessarily set out to change. Congregations seek to accomplish a wonderful goal or fulfill a powerful mission. They set out to learn. They develop new ways of thinking and doing. But congregations that accomplish these things don't do so because they seek to change. After all, change as its own end is a dead end path. Change is a consequence of seeking a better reality. Thus, a theory of change is in actuality a theory of development.

This learning community theory of development for congregations includes the following:

- Congregations learn to do new things when the new thing is something that naturally comes from the community's experience. The initiative needs to be with the congregation, not some other force.
- Congregations learn when they are ready.
- Effective learning is destabilizing, not unlike any number of Jesus's parables that upset the expectations of the listener. How can a mustard shrub

create sufficient shelter (Matt. 13:31–32)? When is a bad Samaritan ever good? Learning involves reversals, disappointment, and challenge.

- Learning is most likely to occur when the challenge is just beyond the capacity of the learner. If it is too easy, nothing is learned. If it is too difficult, frustration gets in the way.
- The congregation makes progress when as a learning community it receives an appropriate ratio of affirmation and challenge. That ratio is something like 5:1 in favor of affirmation.
- Human development and maturity is the learning goal regardless of the subject. The institutional development is the container but not the ultimate end. Richer lives, better people is the end goal.
- Solutions come from both beyond and within.

I know this is not a comprehensive conceptual framework. Yet, it is worthwhile to name values that keep development the focus and not change simply for the sake of change.

Think in terms of increasing congregational capacity rather than in terms of congregational change. Learning congregations will ultimately change in the direction they most need to change. Yet that change will be the result of learning and not because of a change effort. By framing congregational experience in terms of "what are we learning" instead of "this is what we need to change," the community experiences important developmental shifts.

Now, what does your congregation seek to learn? And how are you going to get the help you need to accomplish what you seek to do?

You know you are on a learning journey when the following occur:

- Your congregation is gaining skills to do something it hasn't done before.
- Training isn't enough. You need to draw forth something new from your community of faith.
- You and your colleagues aren't stumped thinking about how to get people to accept change.
- You frame the challenge as something new to learn.

When thinking about your congregation as a learning community it is good to consider the following:

- Which realm the learning most resides in: organizational, religious, or life realms.
- Ways in which learning can be seen as fun and not as tactical work.
- What behavior and emotional adjustments would signify progress for your congregation.
- What you personally want to learn.

Questions to ask when considering congregational learning include the following:

- Where are we on the journey at this moment? Identifying the challenge? Or are we elsewhere on the passage of learning—say, seeking validation?
- What learning behavior is our congregation generally most skilled at? Using an outside resource? The art of conversation? Or one of the others?
- How can we integrate the various realms of learning as we address a challenge?

Chapter Two

Getting the Help You Deserve

Resources and Ingenuity

A congregation begins an arts ministry. The congregation has many artists—talented creators of music, paintings, and poetry. Yet, the congregation has never had a structured arts program. The board sends representatives to three other congregations to learn the particulars of beginning a creative arts ministry. The board members return from their learning expeditions with new ideas, new questions, and two distinct next steps. If they had not sought help, they could still be talking about an arts ministry rather than taking steps to do something.

The need for assistance is not because of an inherent lack in a congregation or some deficiency in the people who lead congregations. It is the opposite. Look at the sports world. The top professional and Olympic athletes have coaches, trainers, advisers, psychologists, consultants, and managers. The business world is similar. The more a leader seeks to accomplish, the more outside resources are needed. The greater a congregation's capacity, the more it is likely to take on difficult challenges. The more difficult the challenge, the more productive it is for a congregation to seek help. Indeed, not seeking help would be a sign of ineffective leadership.

FIND HELP THAT FITS YOUR CONTEXT AND CAPACITY

A pastor speaks:

> When I arrived at the congregation I serve, I learned that the senior pastor was suffering from a mental illness. I was told in no uncertain terms that it was my responsibility to get him help. I was twenty-six years old and just out of

seminary. I told this to a pastoral counselor and the counselor's response was that I was just buying into the congregation's anxiety. The remark wasn't particularly helpful.

Receiving good help is a craft. It is a faith practice as important as offering help. However, there are common pitfalls to accepting help. One pitfall to accepting help is that you feel inadequate. That's not a good feeling. When it comes to helping your congregation, learn to fend off this emotion. Indeed, no one learns without help. Asking for help is a sign of maturity.

If you want your congregation to be less overwhelmed by the demands placed upon it, then it is important to learn how to receive just enough help at the right time and in the right way. Avoid help that is not wanted. It is common to describe a challenge to another person and have that person, well-meaning as she or he might be, offer assistance that doesn't fit what you described. Sidestep assistance that provides too much of what is needed. Receiving help is not the same as dependence. Also, pass over prescribed solutions that do not fit the energy, capacity, or commitment of your congregation.

What are characteristics of enough help at the right time and in the right way? A key characteristic of good help is that the help offered will not only solve a congregational challenge, it will also change you as a person. Find help that leaves you with greater capacity to take risks. If you learn, then it is more likely that others in your congregation will learn from you. As a recipient of help, you will want to find resources that fit your context and extend your capacity at least one increment. How does one measure one increment? Help that you receive should move you to take an action step for the good of the congregation that you otherwise would not have taken.

The help you seek needs to honor the context of your situation. Several years ago, there was a resource available to congregations that was noted as a best practice and recognized as a best seller. Thousands of copies were purchased to share with governing boards across the United States. The Indianapolis Center for Congregations collected narratives to assess the impact the book had on congregations. We found that although many people read the book, almost no congregations applied any of its assertions. The resource wasn't translatable. The help offered was, at best, inspirational.

In another situation, a Roman Catholic parish council was looking for an internal assessment tool. The parish leaders wanted to learn about the council's strengths and weaknesses. The priest said, "We don't know ourselves well enough to reach out." They were comparing three surveys developed by three organizations. One survey asked a question about whether or not parishioners "enjoyed" worship. The priest said, "That question won't work for us. Our liturgy is the work of the assembly. It is for the glory of God. We don't rank enjoyment. At least not in that way." So they knew to move on to the other choices. This is an example of finding help that fits your context.

JUXTAPOSING AN OUTSIDE RESOURCE
WITH YOUR OWN INGENUITY

As a congregational leader you have the best chance of accomplishing good things when you use outside help in concert with your congregation's own creativity. This juxtaposition sparks learning. The congregation's inner creativity includes its theology, polity, and context, plus the talents and assets of its leaders and constituents. The outside resources might be a book, a workshop, a webinar, a website, a consultant, a coach, another congregation, a vendor, a professional with special expertise (like an architect), a video, and so on. The use of an outside resource is key to any congregational learning journey.

In terms of learning, juxtaposition is the act of placing two dynamics together with the contrasting effect leading to a new discovery. Energy flows from the juxtaposition. Discoveries occur as a result of joining outside help with your creativity. Don't give up your agency. Don't relinquish the initiative of your congregation. Apply your gifts. A learning congregation becomes skilled at mixing knowledge gained from an outside resource with the wisdom already present within. A congregation can now act on its challenge, affect its challenge, and reshape it for positive purposes.

A congregation that learns to juxtapose these two dynamics (inner creativity/outside resource) in a learning journey can become not only organizationally sturdier, but also more likely to close the gap between espoused religious claims, commitments, and lived practice. Leaders can construct their own understanding of what will work best in their context. The resource can help move leaders from private opinions to a more comprehensive appraisal of the situation.

Here is an example of juxtaposing a resource with congregational creativity. St. Timothy's Episcopal Church wanted to enhance the experience of young children in worship. The congregation had recently experienced an increase in the sound of children's footsteps in their building. They looked to a popular (and wonderful) resource called *Young Children and Worship*.[1] The teachers and clergy leader, the Rev. Rebecca Nickel, learned much from another, related resource called *Godly Play*.[2] They discovered many positive aspects about this educational approach based on Montessori methods. The children would learn Bible stories. The children would discover meaning in scripture in a setting that had structure; the classroom rituals mirrored rituals in worship. This congregation often had families attending church for the first time, so the spirit of hospitality that was lodged in the curriculum was heartening. However, they wanted to make one significant adaptation. "We want this to shape Lord's Day worship, not just Sunday School," said Rev. Nickel. As a result, she brought the classroom rituals into worship one Sunday a month. The sermon was presented in the style of the curriculum. "The adults lean forward. The place is silent when we tell the story. It is holy time," says Rev. Nickel. She and other leaders effectively took excellent resources and adapted them through the application of their creativity.

A CAUTION IN SEEKING OUTSIDE RESOURCES

Your congregation probably faces the same issues that many congregations face. However, the practice of generalizing or categorizing when it comes to the life of a congregation is of limited value. In seeking an outside resource to assist your congregation on its learning journey, remember that your congregation is unique. There is a careful matching process in which you evaluate the difficulty of the challenge in relationship to the capacity of your congregation. Hence the following words of caution.

There is knowledge that comes from studying groups. Such knowledge is often applied in an overarching fashion to individuals. Public health studies work this way. Trends observed in large populations are translated into interventions for individuals.

Then, there is knowledge that comes from knowing individuals. The psychologist Gordon Allport contrasted these two words, *idiographic* and *nomothetic*, to distinguish between knowledge that categorizes in clusters and knowledge that deciphers what is unique about an individual.[3] These are obscure words. They are important because they represent a nuanced way of thinking about congregational life.

Idiographic means that which is unique. The Greek word *idios* can be translated, "That which is uniquely your own." See Luke 6:44: "For each tree is known by its *own* fruit." The fruit is unlike any other. Or recall the passage in the *Little Prince* where the fox wants the little prince to tame him. If the little prince tames the fox, then, as the fox says, "I'll know the sound of footsteps that will be different from all the rest."[4] This is idiographic thinking.

Nomothetic thinking categorizes broadly. A nomothetic way of thinking would contrast fruit from vegetables. This is helpful when making generalizations. But it is not helpful when wanting to distinguish two fruits from the same branch. Or when seeking to tame a fox.

Nomothetic assessments can be limiting, even discrediting ("your congregation is part of the mainline decline"). Consider that in mental health counseling there is a need for diagnosis in order to have insurance coverage. A diagnostic manual called the *DSM-5* (*Diagnostic and Statistical Manual of*

Mental Disorders) provides criteria for various findings regarding the nature of a psychological illness.[5] Although the diagnosis is essential for insurance reimbursements, the diagnosis also informs the treatment plan. However, a diagnosis can be too general. For example, here are two gentlemen, one named Ted and the other Thomas. They have both been diagnosed with major depression. But their symptoms are different. One of Ted's presenting symptoms is that he can't sleep. One of Thomas's symptoms is that he can't get out of bed. Not only are the symptoms different, the symptoms are entirely opposite. The generalization (the nomothetic diagnosis) has limited value. It can't be the only information the therapist uses to design a treatment plan. A precise or idiographic observation and treatment plan is required to relieve the particular suffering.

The practice of generalizing or categorizing when it comes to the life of a congregation is of limited value. Accurate observations about congregational life are, more than ever before, idiographic rather than nomothetic. The support that will serve your congregation best is related to your ability to know a particular congregation as unique, not like any other. Categorizations related to denomination, size, location, or even theology are no longer specific enough. Any diagnosis or problem definition based on a nomothetic discernment is going to be inadequate. If you seek to help your congregation learn to accomplish wonderful things, become an idiographic thinker.

Let's invite the philosopher Emmanuel Levinas to this discussion. His philosophical framework involves reflection on the human "face," both actual and metaphorical. The uniqueness of a life situation is exemplified not by generalities or by oversimplifications. The uniqueness and therefore true meaning of a life situation is revealed in the face of the other. Meaning comes from knowing up close. Furthermore, meaning is revealed in our affective response to the face of the other. As Bettina Bergo writes, "Otherwise, [meaning] is deduced from principles that have long since been abstracted from the immediacy of the face-to-face encounter with the other."[6] In writing about Levinas, homiletician John McClure describes the dynamic of discovering the "glory of the infinite in the face of the other."[7] Learning begins with the uniqueness of the face that is right in front of you. Learning begins with that which is distinctive, that which is up close and personal, about your situation.

The congregational challenge may be as ordinary as roof repair or as transcendent as teaching mindfulness prayer to autistic children. Regardless, the leader's task in a learning congregation is to observe behavior and interpret meaning based on the unique face of the situation, a situation that is entirely different from one congregation to the next. The best use of an outside resource takes into account the congregation's context. Doing so avoids the common pitfalls of assisting another person or organization: providing what is not wanted, providing too much of what is needed, or prescribing solutions that do not fit the energy, capacity, or commitment of the recipient.

BEST PRACTICES ARE MISLEADING

One implication of all this has to do with best practices. The notion of best practices when it comes to learning from outside resources is misleading. There is a difference between best *practices* and best *principles*. A report by the Union for Reform Judaism titled *Strengthening Congregations: Paving the Road to Meaningful Young Adult Engagement* describes the difference between practices and principles. The authors describe the difference this way:

> Best principles are fundamental elements that one must consider when creating a new initiative or adapting one that exists. They are concepts forged from experience, which must be the framework around which any program is designed. This is not to be confused with best practices. Too often a program is considered a best practice and it is assumed that if you replicate the program you too will garner success in your congregation/institution. We advise that you view the best principles and treat them as the tenets that undergird a program, regardless of what you might want to implement. [8]

There may be such a thing as a best practice for a training situation, such as how to reconcile a church's bank statements. However, there are rarely best practices when it comes to seeking transformation. The best resources help you think more clearly about your own situation and are adaptable to a variety of other contexts. Be wary of the expectation that solutions that worked elsewhere will work for you, too.

For the learning challenges this book addresses, a congregation can find its own choice practice based on reliable principles. A congregation across town has found a way to increase Biblical literacy. The leaders launch an all-congregation effort encouraging small group participants to read through the Bible every other year using a specific curriculum. Using this curriculum may or may not be the best way for your congregation to engage scripture. However, two key principles applied by the other congregation might prove useful. The principles include beginning with the participant's present knowledge of scripture and making sure the leaders are committed to the program because of the amount of time required.

A best principle represents a fundamental, primary idea. A best practice operates at the level of action, in the direct experience of *doing* something. Such actions require consideration of the idiographic (unique) face of the congregation. Because of the singular characteristics—the uniqueness—of a congregation, transferring advice from one setting to another has limited value.

The tendency to generalize help for congregations produces narrow results. It may indeed negate a congregation's relationship to being in the image of God. It may negate a congregation's ability to see the true face of the challenge. The best help is that which seeks understanding based on subjective experience. Two congregations may both be facing a financial crisis. However, one congregation may be experiencing a financial crisis because the area it resides in has high unemployment. The other congregation experiences a financial crisis because it functions from a theology of scarcity related to unfortunate occurrences in the past. Both can be categorized as experiencing financial challenges. But the idiographic nature of their experience is crucial to helping them find an appropriate response.

As you scan the landscape of your challenge to determine the best-fit resources for your learning, keep a list of potential outside helpers. As you use these resources, be sure you adapt them to your situation. Don't let the accessible, supposed solutions of a best practice keep you less engaged. Decide on next steps you take as a result of what you have learned from these resources. These action steps should be consistent with the gifts evident in your congregation. It comes down to names and faces of those in your congregation, not words on a page or a script from a consultant. Action steps need to be as specific as possible, designed for your situation. Don't inhabit an oblique notion of an obscure thought.

HOW TO FIND GOOD RESOURCES

It is not easy to find the best resource for your challenge. Systems of support for congregations are not as strong as they need to be. There was a time when you might have gone to your local judicatory's resource center. There you could find a book on worship to help you consider changes to your liturgy. Now, many resource centers have closed.

Other denominational networks are struggling, too. Budgets for new books and curriculums are not abundant. Denominational staff, who once served as valuable resources to congregational leaders, have retired or moved to new jobs.

Paradoxically, while past delivery systems of resources are declining, there are more resources than ever before for congregations. Though established support networks are disappearing, new networks complete with new resources are available. The abundance of new resources is both good news and bad news. The bad news is that not all the help is useful. In fact, when it comes to your specific issues, very little of the help is going to be a productive match. The good news is that a few guidelines can help you find the help you deserve. Here are some guidelines:

Ask those you trust for resource referrals. If you ask a person who knows you, who knows your congregation, who understands your setting, you are more likely to get resource recommendations that are a match for your challenge.

Yes, use Google. The Internet is an excellent resource center. However, you will need to curate what you find. Often the first thing you find on the Internet isn't going to be the best resource for you, but by extending a string of searches you will learn what is available.

There is an online tool called the Congregational Resource Guide (http://www.thecrg.org). It was developed by my colleagues at the Indianapolis Center for Congregations. It has some sixteen hundred resources curated and annotated about any number of congregational issues. Use it. It will help you not only define your challenge precisely; you will also find any number of resources that will mix with your creativity, moving you closer to discovering a solution.

Look for resources that are recent. There is nothing wrong with a tried and true resource. Yet, the world is changing quickly. A more recent resource is going to be more relevant.

Make sure the resource is trustworthy. You can't expect most congregational resources to represent controlled, university-level research. However, books that tell the miraculous story of one congregation are of limited value to your congregation.

A particular resource may be excellent. But if it doesn't address your challenge then it might move you off the course, and you will be taking a learning journey you had not anticipated. So, a resource needs to address your challenge, your opportunity. Make sure the resource teaches you about the subject you are addressing and not some other topic that might sound similar.

The best resources are practical. Or put another way, they promote the right way to do the right thing.

Is your congregational function a clergy role? I encourage you to add the role of *curate* to how you see yourself. *Curate* is a word that used to describe clergy. Though the word has been used differently in various historical contexts, a curate is one devoted to the care or cure of souls. In recent years the word *curation* (derived from *curate*) has been applied to websites that gather resources about certain subjects. For example, there are many websites that host blogs and other forms of information about medical conditions, hobbies, social services, vocations, and so forth. The act of curation—the gathering and vetting of resources—is helpful to those seeking more information about these subjects. As a clergyperson, you are a curate in terms of the care of souls. You are also a curate in terms of discovering resources that will help your congregation address its challenges and opportunities.

DEVELOPMENTAL REALITY AND LEVELS OF RESOURCES

You can see the building from almost a mile away. It is a brown, brick building with a tall steeple. The building is the home to a congregation located three miles out of town, along an Indiana state road. When you arrive, the first thing you see is the sign board that carries the message, "Can't Sleep? Listen to a Sermon." The pastor greets you at the door. She has served the congregation for four years. It is her first call out of seminary.

When asked, "What's going on?" she folds her arms and starts this story: "The council can't agree and they want me to solve it for them. Some folks want us to raise our mission giving from 6 percent of our budget to 15 percent of our budget. I told them let's see if there is something out there that can help us because we keep disagreeing over the numbers."

The pastor has many options. After all, there is a world of help available to congregations. The pastor could turn to systems theory to understand the problem. She might diagnose the council's plight in terms of relationship triangles or lack of self-differentiation.[9] Or she might look at the decision about money from a therapeutic lens, encouraging the group to share their feelings with the hope that better understanding might result.

There are more options. Our pastor friend might begin by searching "congregational mission giving" on the Internet. She might call pastor friends to see if they have faced this challenge. She might search Amazon for a book on congregational finances or call an organization such as the Church Network, formerly known as the National Association of Church Business Administrators.

Not just any resource will do. As described above, finding the best resource involves honoring what is unique about the congregation. It involves juxtaposition; matching the congregation's creativity with the information the resource has to offer. *And finding the best resource also involves pairing the resource with the developmental reality of the congregation.*

What is the developmental reality of a congregation? Every congregation has the potential to advance. To advance means to accomplish ever more difficult goals in order to fulfill a larger mission. It happens in steps. It can be measured in increments or degrees. Not unlike the way a teenager begins playing a single snare drum, and then in a year is playing a snare and a cymbal, and then soon an entire drum set in a jazz band, so a congregation also grows in its ability.

Through a process of learning that matches capacity (or that actually extends capacity at least one increment forward), congregations can take

hold of their challenges rather than their challenges having a hold on them. [10]
With this language I'm drawing on the work of Robert Kegan and Lisa
Lahey related to the dynamics of human development. They refer to the way
a person can learn to be an active subject in relationship to life challenges
(the object). [11] This can be true for organizations, too. That is, a congregation
can now act on its challenge, affect its challenge, and reshape it for positive
purposes. This is a sign of congregational agency and such agency almost
always signals a positive developmental shift. *Everyone has the right to be
helped in ways over which they have agency.*

The Center for Congregations's first director John Wimmer speaks of the
need for congregations to experience an "inversion of initiative" when it
comes to accomplishing what they seek to do. A congregation most ably
finds solutions to challenges when the initiative is coming from the leaders of
the congregation. Solutions do not emerge when the definition of the challenge is coming from a denomination, or from the government, or from a
cultural movement that temporarily has public attention. Such a position
keeps congregations in a reactive mode—ultimately a passive mode. Rever-
sal of initiative means that the congregation is taking the upper hand in
identifying a challenge and exploring solutions. In this way congregations
are like adult, self-directed learners who have learned to take responsibility
for contructing new approaches to meet the demands they face. Robert Kegan describes this in terms of subject/object relationships. When the challenge is overwhelming, *subject* refers to ideas and experiences that are too
fused with our way of looking at the world. When learning is taking place,
object refers to ideas and experiences that we are able to look at perceptibly
and for which we assume responsibility. [12] Objectivity and responsibility are
conditions that make it possible for congregational leaders to take initiative.
Ideally, congregational leaders originate the work they need to do and assume agency for their own learning. The congregation's agency—its commitment—is a marker of effectiveness.

There is no end to the developmental learning through strategic help
seeking that can take place in a congregation. There is no A+, black-belt
level to be achieved or Eden to be visited. Congregations are always going to
be challenged. Your task is to experience learning designed to extend your
congregation from its current developmental learning stance.

I have observed four levels of domains representing the developmental
reality of a congregation in relationship to outside resources. Each domain
represents the capacity the congregation has in relationship to a particular
challenge.

Do not apply an overall developmental score to your congregation. There
isn't a scale to represent the capacity of a congregation. Just as a violinist
would be challenged by suddenly switching to oboe, so your congregation

functions in a different developmental domain in response to different challenges or opportunities.

Your congregation may function differently while implementing a strategic plan than when dealing with a personnel issue. If you have effectively led your congregation through a planning process, your congregation will be more developmentally advanced in addressing strategic thinking. If your congregation seeks to hire a children's pastor for the first time, it will not be as developed in relationship to this task.

The four observable developmental domains are: information, training, education, and transformation. Each domain implies different conditions and strategies. Your congregation stands in a different place developmentally to each potential challenge. This is important. The reason this is important is that congregational leaders often approach many different challenges with the same developmental frame. This can create a mismatch when it comes to finding the best resource. It can create disappointment when expectations are too high. Just as you wouldn't offer a curriculum of advanced knot theory to a ninth-grade math student, you don't want to create a learning journey that is beyond the capacity of your congregation.

Let's say a pastor wants to begin a support group for families that experience mental illness. If this congregation isn't sure what the objective is yet, or if the idea has only been tested with one other person, and the pastor doesn't have a clear answer when asked how this connects to the mission of the congregation, then it would be premature as well as discouraging to hire a coach to guide the process. The pastor and congregation aren't yet ready for a coach or consultant. It would be better for the pastor to circulate among the board a short article on mental health and ways congregations can support families dealing with mental illness.

You also don't want to underestimate. It can create frustration if you engage a resource that is below your capacity. Say a lay leader wants a prayer ministry to have more impact. She is working with the Spiritual Formation Team to initiate a day once a month in which members of the congregation promise to pray steadfastly in one-hour shifts over twenty-four hours. This involves the sanctuary being open around the clock on the third Thursday of the month. This congregation already has an active prayer ministry. Every year they host a prayer walk for the town. They have sent people to a variety of training sessions on prayer and health. Their mission statement begins, "We are a praying congregation." The strength of the congregation regarding prayer is evident, so this congregation is ready for education and even transformation around prayer. The impact potential is high. It is likely that this congregation might also be able to be a teaching congregation for others when it comes to prayer. Having the board read a simplistic blog on prayer will feel like standing within a predetermined boundary. It would feel restrictive to the leaders. Such a resource would be like giving a Shakespearean scholar a lightweight, poorly written novel to read.

Your congregation functions developmentally differently depending on any number of variables. These variables include several categories.

One category is how you construct the challenge or opportunity. How aware are you of the complete picture of the challenge? Are there parts of the challenge that you don't see clearly? All life challenges, congregational and otherwise, contain elements that you don't see, that you don't understand. Such challenges maintain control over you.[13] There is a congregation that keeps trying to resolve the same issue regarding their staffing situation. So far, no matter what they try, the solutions are unsatisfactory. There is something or some things about this challenge that has control over the congregational leaders. Perhaps the challenge is intractable. Perhaps it is not. The challenge is overwhelming to the point that leaders do not stand in objective relationship to it.

As you gain more expertise your view of a challenge changes. You talk about it differently. You hold the challenge with more confidence, greater clarity. You are able to exert influence over the challenge. You are ready for deeper learning experiences. You can move from seeking information to seeking training and education because you have assumed more responsibility for the challenge. You see it more accurately and clearly. It is no longer just in your peripheral vision. It is us up front and center and you can now work on it.[14]

Another category is the fit of the challenge to your congregation's overall mission. When I listen to clergy and laity describe a challenge I pay attention to whether or not the challenge is described in relationship to the congregation's purpose. Of course, not every congregation issue relates to a deeper purpose. Sometimes the challenge is to just get the furnace fixed. Yet, more times than not a congregational challenge is like the geometric figure called a fractal. A fractal is a smaller set that reveals patterns evident at larger scales. Each part, or set, of a congregation represents in some way the character of the whole. The more this is made explicit in talking about a challenge, the more the challenge—if addressed effectively—will have a comprehensive positive effect on the congregation. To test this dynamic, listen for whether or not others describe a specific congregational opportunity in light of the congregation's overall stated purpose. The more congruence between the "smaller" challenge and the overall purpose, the more capacity will be gained by successfully addressing the "smaller" issue.

Who are you talking to? How many people are involved? I'm talking to a lay leader who has called about money problems in the church. When I ask who else he has talked to, he answers, "No one really, just somebody at the coffee shop. Their church has money issues, too." This tells me that the lay leader, and probably other leaders in the congregation, needs some introductory learning about church finances. They aren't ready yet to change the culture of the congregation regarding faith and giving because the number of conversation partners is too small. Who and how many people are involved in the conversation indicate congregational capacity. High-level transformation requires focused conversation between clergy and laity with both formal and informal influence. As a congregation moves from seeking information to seeking training, education, and ultimately transformation, the number of people involved in the conversation is likely to increase.

How do you think about the challenge in relationship to your primary religious claims and commitments? Some congregations are gifted at talking about their challenges using the language of faith. Some congregations are able to describe their opportunities in terms of long held values. Such ability demonstrates that congregational leaders are able to integrate the sometimes mundane, practical concerns of congregational operations with the larger landscape of a religious worldview. When the language of faith and the language of values are applied to how a challenge is discussed, that is a signal that the congregation has capacity to address the issue in such a way that something new is going to be discovered.

The way a congregation uses an outside resource reveals capacity. How you use the outside help to address the challenge or opportunity demonstrates your readiness. For instance, a large suburban congregation is beginning a conversation about sharing their building with an immigrant population. They receive an article about some basic "dos and don'ts." A month later the article remains as an unopened attachment in the original e-mail. This is a sign that the congregational leaders aren't ready yet to begin to consider the subject.

Remember Maslow's hierarchy of needs?[15] Picture a pyramid. At the bottom of the pyramid are the most basic needs. They include biological and physiological needs. Then farther up the pyramid there are needs such as safety and stability. Farther up one finds belonging and affinity groups. At the top of the pyramid you will see self-actualization, which includes personal growth and fulfillment.

There is also a hierarchy of resources. I first thought about this when George Bullard of the Columbia Partnership provided a consultation with the Center for Congregations. Rev. Bullard sketched out a ranking of resource type corresponding with the capacity of the congregation. At the bottom of the list was a short article or a blog. At the top of the list was a coach. I've adapted Rev. Bullard's thinking and created a hierarchy of resources based on the domains of capacity that I've observed in congregations. The ranking of the resource type looks like this:

Domain One—Information: an article, a blog, a chart. At this level of readiness, the congregational leaders seek basic facts. Leaders benefit from data. Specific, concrete direction is helpful.

Domain Two—Training: an appropriate book or book chapter, a training session, a conversation with another congregation that has done something very similar. Training includes being shown how to do something (think of training about how to use software or how to conduct an interview). Training includes practice that improves proficiency.

Domain Three—Education: A workshop, a conference, a consultant, contact with another congregation that is thinking about something very similar. Education draws something new out of the participants. Judgment is enhanced.

Domain Four—Transformation: An extended learning experience, a coach, contact with another congregation that is fundamentally changing because of a challenge. With transformation, something essential is not only learned, but the learning also converts the form of the congregation in some important way.

Knowing where your congregation is developmentally in relationship to any specific challenge can help leaders make wise decisions about learning to address the challenge more effectively. Below I describe the four domains in greater detail.

Domain One—Information

A congregation seeks help about a challenge or opportunity that is not well defined. In this case, the challenge is not tied to the congregation's overall mission. Often only one or two people from the congregation seek resources. The challenge as stated is overwhelming to the congregation. Congregational leaders and members do not talk about the challenge in terms of their religious claims and commitments. In conversation, it is difficult for leaders to discern the dynamics of power and love at work in the congregation. Responses to questions about the challenge are deflected. Recommendations are typically not acted upon. For example, a book may be offered by a clergyperson but none of the laity read it. Or a report might be made by a lay leader or by the pastor and other leaders don't have much to say in response. Resources have not opened up creative space between the challenge and the congregation. At subsequent meetings progress is reported to be at a standstill. When these behaviors are evident, the congregation is not ready to take on the challenge. Or they need to start with a simple resource, a short article or a blog. They need to act incrementally with their learning until they are engaged and their creativity (ingenuity) kicks in.

Domain Two—Training

A congregation seeks help about a challenge that is somewhat defined. The challenge is not necessarily tied to the congregation's larger mission (though occasionally it is). There may be some reference to religious claims and commitments, though such reference may not be relevant. The dynamics of power may be more apparent than the dynamics of love. The congregation is seeking a solution or an answer. Sometimes leaders will look to an outside resource and say "tell us what to do." Living in this domain, useful forms of help tend to be resources that are directive, clear, and have been tried before. Useful resources provide objective space between the congregation and its challenge so that the congregation has room to act. Often forms of training or talking to a congregation that has been in a similar situation are helpful. It is at this level of capacity, domain two, that a congregation is most likely to find best practices helpful, but in a limited way. If the resource recommendation provides direction and there are a reasonable number of interested people in the congregation working on the challenge, the resource will open up enough space between the congregation and the issue so that *something* happens. Space, in this case, means the degree to which the congregation is able to objectively hold the issue and explore it from different perspectives. At this level, there is typically some space, though limited, for objective consideration. A congregation that effectively receives training will find something is solved, even if temporarily. In the future, the challenge will once again gain the attention of leaders when the former solution no longer holds.

Domain Three—Education

A congregation seeks help about a challenge that is well defined yet may change along the way. The challenge is tied, in a coherent way, to the identity of the congregation. Leaders know what they seek. The congregation knows what it is not after. Typically, an empowered team or a concerned board is involved in finding an outside resource that will support the congregation's own creativity. The congregational leaders want to figure out the challenge or opportunity, and they want outside help, but they also want to figure it out in a way that makes sense in relationship to the congregation's mission and their context. Religious claims and commitments are described and examples are often given. The dynamics of power and love within the congregation are apparent, considered, and leaders are conscious of the balance or imbalance of these dynamics. Often a variety of resources is helpful, including educational experiences, in-depth books and websites, consultants, or coaches. These resources open up much opportunity space for the congregation. The congregation is an active agent in its own learning. The leaders don't cede too much power to the resources; instead, the resources are adapted to the particular context. Different people in the congregation hold various roles and functions in the learning process. These learning roles and functions are. typically well defined. The process takes time. Even when things are slow it is a creative, engaging time. The congregation initiates much of the contact with the helpers. The congregation offers its appraisal about how it is doing. The learning process not only addresses the challenge, but also advances new knowledge in the congregation. Often, something about the learning process in addressing this challenge or opportunity can be adapted to the next challenge they choose to address. When a congregation is operating out of this domain, deep exploration (and learning) is taking place.

Domain Four—Transformation

A congregation seeks help about a challenge that is well defined. The challenge may change along the way. The task is tied to the identity of the congregation. It is linked to a larger purpose beyond the congregation. There is something transcendent about the challenge and its relationship to the congregation. Religious claims and commitments are described, examples are given, and the examples are stories from the congregation. The dynamics of power and love within the congregation are apparent, considered, and conscious, and love is at the helm even if it means risk and sacrifice. The congregation may be using more of its internal gifts, talents, and knowledge than an outside resource (though outside resources are used). Or it is using several different kinds of resources in unique ways. The congregation tells a rich, full story about the experience and the story expresses much about the religious claims and commitments of the congregation. The experience of the congregation often proves helpful to other congregations. A congregation operating in this domain of learning is likely to become frustrated if the next challenge isn't as carefully addressed. This is because solving a previous challenge has changed the form of the congregation; it is now different. The difference may be in the congregation's culture, in the values it holds, or in some quandary related to faith, power, and love. The difference is not unlike a teenager moving into young adulthood. The person has not just grown taller; the person also sees the world differently. He or she takes a different view of the world into their daily interactions. So, a congregation that has experienced a change of form in this sense will experience frustration if the change isn't sustained. This will at first be disconcerting. Yet, if the congregation can slow down and reflect on past learning experiences, it will gather up its inner wisdom to increase its capacity to face any number of issues.

OPEN SYSTEM VERSUS CLOSED SYSTEM

To what extent is your congregation an open system or closed system when it comes to learning? An open system is one in which you and other leaders look to outside resources for help and in which you also look for resources that come from beyond the congregational world. A closed system means that you are hesitant to trust, to spend for, and to learn from outside resources and that, when you do, you stay within the arena of congregational life.

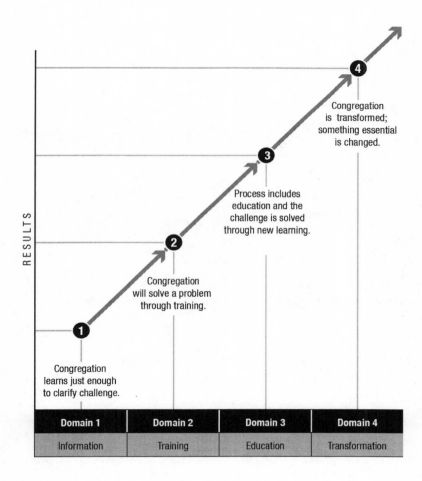

Figure 2.1. Developmental Domains. Developmental domains represent the capacity of a congregation in relationship to any particular challenge. The present capacity of the congregation informs what kind of resource or learning initiative is needed.

	Domain 1	Domain 2	Domain 3	Domain 4
	Information	Training	Education	Transformation
Hierarchy of Resources	Article, Blog	Book, Workshop, Another Congregation	Conference, Consultant	Long term Learning, Coach
Construction of Challenge	Not well defined. Little or no subject/object differentiation between congregation and challenge/ opportunity.	Somewhat defined. A little subject/ object differentiation between congregation and challenge, opportunity.	Well defined. Good subject/object definition and resource will provide even more. Issue may change.	Well defined. Excellent subject/object differentiation. Often linked to larger purpose beyond congregation itself.
People Involved	One or two people involved.	One or two people involved, talking to others who know of the challenge, opportunity.	Functioning team or engaged board at work. Clear roles and functions.	Relationships of those involved show love and respect even if it means risk and sacrifice.
Connection to Overall Mission	Little or no connection to overall mission.	Some, often implicit, connection to overall mission.	Evident connection to overall mission.	Explicit connection to mission, often linked to larger purpose beyond congregation itself.
Relationship to Religious Claims and Commitments	Little or no reference to religious claims and commitments.	Some reference to religious claims and commitments, not necessarily contextual.	Noticeable reference to religious claims and commitments, probably contextual.	Comprehensive reference to religious claims and commitments, highly contextual.
Use of Outside Resource	What's the issue? Article remains or blog shared with others.	Tell us what to do. Looking for a resource that will fix the problem.	Resource helps draw something new from congregation. A variety of resources are used.	Congregation may use more of its internal gifts than an outside resource, or adapt several resources.
Result	Congregation learns just enough to clarify challenge.	Congregation will solve a problem through training.	Process includes education and the challenge is solved through new learning.	Congregation is transformed; something essential is changed.

Figure 2.2.   Developmental Domain Grid. This grid represents the characteristics held by a congregation in relationship to what it seeks to learn. The type of learning, the kind of resource that best fits the congregation, can be determined by how leaders construct the challenge, the number of people involved, and so forth.

There is a positive correlation between congregations doing new things effectively and seeking help apart from the congregational world. It helps if the congregation views God as active in creation beyond ecclesial structures. Congregational leaders who view secular culture as effectively against Christian faith will have greater difficulty functioning as an open system when it comes to congregational learning.

What does an open system approach look like? Let us say that certain church leaders from an evangelical congregation wanted to serve the children growing up in a trailer park near their church. Many of the children experience trials at home. There is, sadly, a high rate of domestic violence in the trailer park. Drugs are bought and sold on front porches. Many children miss school because no adult is home early in the morning. The pastor had training in substance-abuse counseling, yet he knew that he and other leaders needed more support and additional skills. The pastor reached out to a public university that had many undergraduate and graduate students in social work. Working with a professor at the school, the congregation's outreach team designed a class project that involved students working with church staff and volunteers in supporting the children. The children's absentee rate from school went down. They started hanging out at the church. The outreach team learned new helping skills. "We know God's world is larger than our little congregation," says the pastor.

In this scenario, the pastor had an open system view when it came to getting the help his congregation needed.

Congregational leaders—clergy and laity alike—benefit from learning with others in the larger community beyond the congregation. Clergy peer groups should give way to leader peer groups in which clergy learn alongside school teachers, other nonprofit leaders, entrepreneurs, nurses, technicians, and so forth. Those that support congregations—for example, seminaries, foundations, outdoor ministries—also need to operate in open systems. God has created a world abundant with helpers. A clergy person wanting to learn more about congregational finances sits down with a banker. A layperson who leads a support group for people suffering from depression consults with a psychiatrist. The governing board wanting to streamline its decision making has a half-day retreat with the governing board of a nonprofit that works to relieve homelessness. These are all are ways in which congregational leaders learn from an open system point of view.

RESOURCES ARE THE KEY

Resources are the key to congregational learning. The use of a resource helps you move your congregation along the phases of a learning journey. Resources help you improve your use of the important elements of a learning journey such as the art of conversation, making good use of rites of passages, discerning the timing of moving forward, and so forth.

Look for resources that do more than reinforce your opinion. Look for resources that keep your congregation from dwelling on its past. Look for helpers who aid you in discerning the relationship between your thinking and your actions. Change your thinking, and you are more likely to change your behavior. Paul's ancient wisdom in Romans 12:2 holds: *Do not be conformed to this world, but be transformed by the renewing of your minds, so that you may discern what is the activity of God—what is good and acceptable and whole.* The best way to keep things the way they are is to focus exclusively on talking about problems rather than thinking through actionable solutions. Seek help that will change behavior.

Help for congregations is often too general. Too often it consists of truisms. *Be more collaborative. Begin with the end in mind. Strive for transparency.* Such nonspecific axioms have the effect of providing a solution to a question that doesn't apply.

The most effective helpers for your congregation will help you clarify your challenge, discern possible solutions, focus on your context, improve in-the-moment behaviors, and prepare you for the inevitable disappointment that happens in most learning endeavors.

The action of seeking help is an educational experience. Your congregation has challenges. It is your calling to address them. Be the learner-in-chief of your faith community. You and your congregation deserve good help and the best opportunity to address the challenges that are part of living a meaningful life together.

You know you are getting the help you deserve when the following occurs:

• Your congregation uses an outside resource in concert with your creativity.
• You seriously consider the best principles of the resources you are using while adapting practices that fit the specific situation of your congregation.
• You look deeply into the face of the challenge, and deeply into the face of those you are working with and seeking to serve.
• You are helped in ways over which you maintain agency.

When seeking an outside resource, it is good to consider

• the level of capacity you have.
• whether you need—at this time—information, training, education, or transformation.
• the benefits of looking outside your typical community of helpers.

- whether the resource potentially enhances your capacity just enough to move you to the next level of learning.

Questions to ask when seeking a resource include the following:

- Does this resource directly address the challenge identified, or is it really about something else?
- Does the resource allow us to adapt its principles to our unique situation?
- In what ways does the resource help us get a hold of the challenge rather than the challenge having a hold on us?
- Is the resource compatible with our theological worldview?
- Who else can we share this resource with so that our circle of learners can expand?

Chapter Three

Challenge

Articulating What You Need to Learn

Sunday School for children was dead. That was what the Rev. Teri Thomas of Northminster Presbyterian Church knew. No longer was the congregation going to host a group of twelve fourth graders in a classroom early on Sunday morning. They weren't going to be sitting at a table with the *Good News Bible* opened to Genesis 1. There wasn't going to be a teacher standing in the room referring to a curriculum prepared by the denomination. It hadn't happened for a while. It wasn't going to happen again. Sunday School as Rev. Thomas had known it was no more.

Rev. Thomas was identifying a challenge facing Northminster Presbyterian Church. This wasn't a challenge that she read about in a book and now was bringing to her board. It wasn't a challenge projected upon the congregation by an outside entity like the local judicatory. It was a challenge coming directly from the life of this congregation.

Many others in the congregation knew this. Not everyone, of course. Yet, there were enough people at Northminster who knew the current state of Sunday School to feel unease about the situation. The dis-ease must have had an element of nostalgia to it. The dis-ease must have had an element of grief to it. Certainly there was a time at the church when there were twelve fourth graders sitting in a classroom learning how God had called creation good. There is a long history of why a classroom-oriented, public-school model of Sunday School is a good thing. Historically it is linked to literacy. Historically it is linked to the personal development of young people. For years—yes, decades—such a Sunday School model was the way children were introduced to the grand narrative of God's involvement with this world. So, grieving and nostalgia had to be part of the congregation's unease with the current reality.

But there also was a future. It was just that the future direction had not been revealed. Rev. Thomas instinctively knew that a way forward was to help the congregation define the challenge before them. Although Sunday School attendance was negligible, the congregation included many children and youth ready for a new experience of learning. So, Rev. Thomas began testing a succinct way of describing the challenge. She tested an evocative question with others. *Sunday School has died. Can we bury it and see what might rise from the ashes?*

Before your congregation can accomplish something new, you need to define your challenge. Ultimately naming the challenge is less a statement and more a distinct phase of the learning journey. Identifying and formulating the challenge involves gathering stories and then crafting words that describe the situation, testing and refining the words used to describe the challenge, and holding off on seeking a solution. You might use a succinct statement. You might use an evocative question. Among fundamental behaviors that will help you in this phase are the art of conversation, measured pace, outside resources, and leadership and learning. Let's explore these dynamics of the challenge part of the learning journey.

THE DISCOMFORT OF DIAGNOSIS

If the challenge is worth addressing, if it involves learning something new, then naming the challenge accurately will create discomfort. Certainly the unease may already be present in the congregation. The naming of the challenge simply, or not so simply, makes the information more explicit. Just as in medicine, diagnosis can provide important yet uncomfortable information. The news can be upsetting.

In medicine, it is crucial to receive the correct diagnosis. Dr. Jerome Groopman, professor of medicine at Harvard University, describes the eighteen-second rule.[1] That's the amount of time, on average, that physicians listen to a patient before deciding on a diagnosis. Doctors are accurate about 85 percent of the time.[2] Based on my observations, congregational leaders have a lower accuracy percentage than physicians. I see the initial accuracy rate to be around 50 percent. A building issue is mistaken for a financial issue. A staff performance challenge is misidentified as a program issue. Sometimes the description is inaccurate because the challenge is a moving target. The description of the challenge is almost always going to change over time. However, there is a difference between the nature of the challenge changing because of iterative learning and the challenge being named incorrectly at the start. Let's look at the process of identifying a worthy challenge for your congregation.

Remember St. Timothy's from chapter 2. This is the congregation that wanted to enhance the worship experience for children. That wasn't how the challenge was originally framed. At first, the challenge was framed, understandably so, as a discipline issue. The children had a difficult time sitting still for worship. It was difficult for the clergyperson and congregation to concentrate on God when the children needed so much attention. ("These children know just how to get to me!" said Rev. Nickel.) With a positive, intuitive sense of discernment, Rev. Nickel knew this was ultimately more than a discipline issue. This was a faith issue. She reframed the conversation with others from discipline to spiritual development and the commitment of the congregation to teach children.

Unease, desire, and purpose are dynamics that contribute to a well-defined challenge.

It starts with a sense of unease. Something isn't quite right. Or something could be better. There is a dent in creation and it has come to your faith community. Sunday School is dying, or maybe the neighborhood has no connection to the congregation. The developmental growth of a congregation (or any human community) begins at the same place the developmental growth of an individual does. It begins with discomfort. Even in the circumstances when the challenge holds possibility, it still takes a communal experience of unease for people to be willing to put in the hard work that follows.

This sense of unease is not the same as urgency. A sense of urgency often is accompanied by congregational anxiety. Such anxiety can narrow the vision of leaders resulting in an inaccurate diagnosis of the situation. Some experts on change describe the need for urgency. Harvard professor John Kotter advocates for the importance of corporations to produce the experience of urgency in order to accomplish a change effort.[3] That is not what I mean by unease. Kotter's framework begins with creating a sense of urgency by getting people to feel the need for change. Urgency creates an imperative for immediate action. It is like a tornado is swirling toward your home. You need to get to the basement *now*! That's urgency. Without it, Kotter contends, complacency is the default stance of businesses.

Creating urgency may be productive in corporations. In the business world it is an imperative to make changes in order to compete. Creating a sense of urgency in congregations (note the word "creating") typically serves to increase defenses and manifest anxiety.

Urgency may be a positive factor in change efforts. However, it is not a positive factor in *learning* efforts. The sense of unease is usually enough motivation. Urgency denotes speed, the need for swift action. Learning is rarely assisted by speed. Unease, on the other hand, denotes discontent. It develops naturally. It isn't produced artificially. A congregation can abide with its discontent as a spiritual discipline. As a result, the challenge will become more clear and described more exactly.

The goal is learning to do new things consistent with the congregation's purpose. A sense of unease is sufficient discomfort. There is no need to manufacture urgency. After all, the sense of unease is another way of expressing desire. Any congregation that sees itself as a learning community will want to explore what a theology of desire sounds and looks like. I learn new things, a hobby such as photography, or something existential, such as how to be more at peace inside my own body, because I hold a sense of longing or hope. I seek a certain outcome. I desire to experience something of which I am not yet capable.

The same is true for congregations. Pay attention to desire, longing, and yearning. These are friends of learning.

In the early experience of addressing a congregational challenge, the unease is often expressed as asides in conversation. A learning endeavor is often inaugurated because of a sidebar conversation—a casual comment, an innocent question. A pastor stands with a layperson at the front door of the church when a train of school buses passes by: "If only we had a way to know more people in our community." Or, in the middle of a conversation about the food pantry, someone might ask, "How many of us remember the first names of those who come to us?" The desire (not urgency) is expressed indirectly, almost as a parenthetical. A sign of learning-oriented leadership is the ability to listen for such comments. The arena of purposeful congregational learning is often described indirectly, as asides in conversations. The pearl of great price is hidden inside a shell (Matt. 13:45–46).

What do you do with such comments? Because the hint of a learning endeavor is often subtly expressed, it requires explicating the asides that come up in multiple conversations. This means lingering with these seemingly insignificant comments. A group lingers (think of lingering as a Sabbath act, not being in a hurry) with these comments when someone in the group draws attention to the comment and invites further consideration.

A person in the group may say, "Let's back up a moment and think about what Frank said. Do we know the names of people who come to the food pantry?" Such an invitation can be offered by anyone in the group. Designated leaders like pastors and chairpersons serve the community well when they take the responsibility to draw the group back to such conversations. Congregations are blessed when others—unofficial leaders—have this gift. Note that such attention is not the same as creating urgency. However, it does provide those in the conversation the space to stay with the potential discomfort long enough to learn something, making the implicit more explicit. It may be disquieting to acknowledge that one does not know the names of those one serves. But that discomfort is not meant to subdue. It is meant to provide a blessed space for learning something. It is the beginning of naming a worthwhile challenge.

IDENTIFYING A CHALLENGE

Identifying a challenge is an essential phase of a congregation's learning to accomplish something new. It often comes at the beginning of a learning journey.

Your congregation faces a number of challenges at any given time. You don't have to manufacture a challenge. What is necessary is to name the challenge correctly and to learn about the correct challenge. Regardless of the size of your congregation, there are many possible challenges to address. Regardless of your congregation's size, you can only take on so many challenges at once. The capacity for focus does not differ as much as you would think from a small congregation to a mega-sized congregation. If the challenge is difficult enough to require learning, then most congregations can only take on three or fewer such challenges at any given time. Therefore, it is important to identify the challenges that are essential enough to elicit time and attention. For Northminster (introduced above), the religious education of young people was such a challenge.

For your congregation to learn how to do something important, it is essential that you state the challenge clearly and simply. The challenge is complex enough. It is not helpful for the definition of the challenge to be confusing. Your understanding of the challenge may change over time. It will if the learning is worthwhile. However, just because you do not have the full picture in focus is not enough reason to delay testing statements about the challenge. It is better to name the challenge and to change it later than it is to not describe the challenge. Storytelling, creating a succinct statement about the challenge, and forming an evocative question are ways to not only work on identifying the challenge, but also to communicate it to others.

ELICITING STORIES

Remember the gospel writer John's description of Jesus addressing a man blind since birth. The disciples' diagnosis centered on sin—the man's or the parent's. Jesus interpreted the situation differently. He reconfigured the encounter as an opportunity to reveal God's desire for wholeness. The way in which a challenge is framed makes a difference. The framing influences mood. It influences the choice of outside resources. The way in which a challenge is expressed shapes the theological values brought to bear on the issue. Finding the right words to describe the challenge is as important as landing on the right challenge to address.

When you have a sense that a new challenge is developing for your congregation, start eliciting stories. Soon you and other leaders will need to be telling a story about the challenge. Before you can do that, you need to listen to others tell stories about the challenge.

Why stories? Stories set context. They make the challenge about something unique. You no longer are talking about just any congregation dealing with a common congregational issue. Generalities are no longer driving the conversation. You are talking about the people others know and care about. A congregation seeking to address homelessness can talk about the issue of homelessness. Or, more effectively, congregants can tell stories about the homeless people they know: Jan, Stephen, and Michelle. Stories give meaning to data. They prompt emotional *and* cognitive responses. They will help you get clear about exactly what the challenge is.

If you don't have a story you don't have a challenge worthy of a learning journey. Expressing the challenge in story form also invites others to join the effort. Stories, as opposed to assertions, reduce defenses and increase curiosity. Your congregation will be more willing to learn if defenses are lowered. Your congregation will be more willing to learn if curiosity is heightened. Stories are essential to learning. They are natural to the congregational environment because so many religious traditions are rooted in scriptural narrative.

When you ask others to tell a story about congregational life, they will often respond with something other than a story, something more like a statement or an opinion. Often what is offered is an example or an anecdote, expressions far short of a story. Perhaps we have been shaped too much by quick video images that convey ideas but not stories. We may have been born as natural storytellers, but many of us have lost the knack. The word "narrative" is misused nowadays. Commentators talk about a candidate's political "narrative" as if they are referring to a story. They are not. They are referring to an opinion the public has about a candidate. Or they are talking about an image the candidate wants to project about his or her campaign. This usage of narrative is not the same as a story.

Say the challenge is related to building a new sanctuary because the present sanctuary has severe engineering flaws. If you were in a group with parishioners where a story was requested, then it is likely that someone would first offer a statement, such as, "Well, we certainly were surprised when we received the report from the engineer."

Or perhaps an opinion would be voiced, such as, "We don't have the money to be even talking about a new sanctuary right now."

The real learning happens, however, when you prompt people to tell about an experience regarding the issue. Statements and opinion may be elements of a story. But, without the details, such elements sound flat and don't provide the real action behind the facts.

A story has the following elements:

- characters
- challenge related to a quest or a goal
- movement in time either forward or backward or both
- a key moment
- resolution or partial resolution of the challenge
- some change in the characters as a result of the experience

Statements and opinion have few of the elements of a story. As a result, little or no learning takes place when the conversation gets stuck without a story. If the task is to tell the story about the challenge the congregation faces regarding the status of the sanctuary, for example, what you are looking for is something like this:

Years ago we needed more space. Our building was built in 1888. We had a beautiful sanctuary but no place for kids and youth to meet for education or youth activities. *We needed space for Sunday School or Sunday School was going to be dead and buried.* Plus we were landlocked downtown. So, one day, Eloise Johnson (let's call her) told the council she wanted to build a basement. This was 1970 and people looked at her like she was John Kennedy back from the dead telling us we were going to Mars. We told her to come back with a plan (thinking she couldn't do it). But I guess folks didn't know Eloise very well.

At the next meeting she had it all planned out, even down to where she was going to rent the heavy equipment. The council said fine, but who is going to do it? Eloise said she was going to get men and women (she emphasized *women*) from all over town to help. Someone said, "You mean you are going to get Baptists and Catholics to build our basement."

"Oh," she said, "they are going to *want* to help us."

So they went to work. It took them one month during the hot summer of 1970. She had people from all walks of life working machinery, digging, putting up footers. And by fall we had ourselves a finished basement and many more friends in the community. Someone said, "This is not the same Eloise Johnson I used to know." (Eloise had been known as one who could not get a dinner planned let alone a basement finished.)

There was only one problem, and no one is blaming Eloise for this, but it was not long after that cracks started to show up in the sanctuary walls. I don't think anyone put together the digging out of the basement and the cracks in the walls. For years, we just plastered and painted over the cracks.

But you know, the first thing the engineer asked four months ago had to do with the basement, "Was the basement part of the original building?" No. We all knew that. But now it seems that the basement, or the result of the basement, is shaping our future plans. Because the next word out of the engineer was, "I'm afraid you aren't long in this building."

This is a full story. It is more than an anecdote or an opinion. It involves a challenge. It reveals a beloved character. It denotes the ambivalence the congregation feels about two realities: the accomplishment related to the basement and the bad news about the present condition of the building. A comprehensive story like this will help you learn what is most important about the challenge. It will direct you to where your energy is most needed. You will more likely find where people sense God at work in a challenge through a story. Such a story will result in people's thinking (and feeling) more fully about the learning journey.

You can elicit stories about a challenge by simply asking for them. *Tell me about a time when our congregation identified a significant building issue.* You can do this one-on-one with people. You can do this in a group. Or you can invite people to share stories in groups of two or three. Your role is as host for the stories. You want to sustain and support these stories for the group. Listen actively. Offer back what you are hearing. Ask the group what themes are present in the stories. These activities are helping the group gain clarity about what is driving the sense of unease. At first the stories may be varied. Not all will be on target. That is exactly the reason why you seek stories. You are seeking to use real life examples to narrow the scope of the challenge so that it is manageable.

You can elicit a story by asking an entire group to create a story. You do this as a group activity. You tell people that you want the group to create the story, about, say, how we've come to this situation with the sanctuary. You begin with, "Once upon a time . . . " and you ask who wants to continue. You guide the story along a timeline. Make sure everyone has an opportunity to add to the narrative in order to invite diverse points of view and increase the number who own the challenge.

How do you get people to tell more than a statement or not get stuck on their own opinions? How can you help them create the story? Let's say you invite a team or your board to tell the story and what you first receive is a short summary.

Years ago we needed more space. So we decided to dig a basement. It went really well. And was lots of fun. And we ended up with lots more room for Sunday School.

The goal is to build upon this. Accept this blurb but treat it as only the beginning or the summary. You build upon it by asking questions (and keeping as silent as possible for the group's thinking to be translated into narrative).

Questions include things like these:

- Who was the go-to person for this?
- What did he/she do next?
- What happened first?

- What was the turning point?
- What problems did you encounter?
- When did you encounter those problems?
- What got solved? And who solved it?
- So tell me again, what was the goal?
- When did the congregation know this was going to work?
- How did the congregation know this was going to work?
- What is still unsolved about this experience?

By nudging the group to create a story, you have created a common experience around the challenge. You and others are learning together.

Expand the circle. The story should no longer be held solely by, say, a building committee. The story now can travel along the learning journey to other staff, to other teams or committees, to the board, and to whomever it makes sense to hear it in your congregational culture. You recruit others to join the journey through the story.

After eliciting stories about the challenge, it is time to simplify and clarify the learning challenge. That is accomplished by creating a succinct question or statement that precisely names the challenge. Crafting the challenge earlier would be premature. As with most good pilgrimages, learning requires preplanning and careful reflection. The learning journey is not a spur-of-the-moment road trip. It is time to simplify that which has been complex. This is a process that will be repeated several times during the learning journey, moving from complexity to clarity. When you are defining your challenge, the move from complexity to clarity involves moving from story to succinct statement.

MOVING FROM STORY TO STATEMENT

Sometime in the third century, a Rabbi named Simlai took up the task of accounting for the number of commandments in Hebrew scripture. He counted 613.[4] Not all agree on his method of counting, but for many at least, the number stands as an accurate accounting.

Not only the number of laws, but also the meaning of the laws are debated. In fact, debate is seen as a healthy, even needed, aspect of the Jewish religion. Debate is a form of education, just as Socratic dialogue is a form of education. The tradition of debate among Jewish teachers is pushed even farther. Reasoned argument is the path to knowledge.

Even the most rigorous debaters acknowledge that ultimately complex arguments need to be clarified so that lessons can be held and life can be lived. The challenge must be concise so that it can be shared broadly and understood unambiguously. Otherwise action is hindered.

The commandments themselves might be succinct summaries of complex and ambiguous narratives. The stories of creation, Eden, Cain and Abel, Abraham and Sara, and oppression under the Pharaoh shaped Israel as a community. Such stories also raised questions. Some of the questions were answered through the Ten Commandments. Think of each commandment as an answer to or summary of a story. Hold each commandment as a response to some question, some challenge raised by a longer narrative. The concise commandments are another step along the learning journey of solving any number of life predicaments. The movement is from experience to story to commandment.

So it is with your congregation. When on a learning journey, you are moving from an experience to a sense of unease, to story gathering, to becoming astute at creating a purposeful and condensed articulation of reality. Such articulation results in a clearly stated challenge that a congregation can learn about and about which it can ultimately do something positive.

Congregations that effectively reach their goals succinctly express their learning purpose, often in one sentence. This first involves getting a clear picture of the challenge by telling a full and winsome story about the congregation's experience. Then leaders need to interpret the story. Just as one interprets scripture, congregational stories about a challenge need to be understood. What themes exist? What patterns repeat? What strengths are apparent? What meaning is contained in the narrative? Interpreting the story or stories about the challenge will bring to light a theme related to the challenge. Almost always a clear topic will emerge. A subject to be addressed will be revealed.

However, it is important for a congregation not to rush to a premature interpretation of the challenge. A statement of the challenge arrived at too soon is almost always unhelpful. That is why this chapter describes the various prerequisite exercises. It is also why it is important to tell a more complex story first and then draw from that story a specific theme that can be expressed in an action-oriented learning statement.

In congregations that effectively accomplish what they set out to do, there is a form to such statements. The form is a compound sentence. For example, the first part of the statement is what you seek to do. *We seek to . . .* This is strengthened by adding a word: *We seek to **learn** . . .* Remember, when your challenge is constructed as a learning endeavor the potential for resistance is lowered. Curiosity increases.

The second part of the statement describes why you want to pursue this endeavor. Such a statement associated with Northminster's Sunday School challenge might be this: *We seek to learn to develop a new model of Sunday School in order to give our children the gift of faith.* It is important to describe what needs to be learned. It is equally important to describe the purpose of the challenge. The "in order to" (or "so that") phrase accentuates intention. It links the challenge to a purpose. What needs to be accomplished is more attainable when congregational leaders are clear about the task at hand and the overall purpose.

The reality is that many congregations do not accomplish what they seek to do because leaders do not know or cannot clearly describe the assignment. Sometimes this is because the challenge hasn't unfolded enough. It isn't clear because there isn't sufficient information. Or sometimes leaders haven't had sufficient experience with the discomfort related to the issue. Sometimes lack of identification and clarity is because the challenge is too close to those involved. It is so much easier to define an appropriate challenge looking in from the outside than from the pulpit you've preached from for ten years. This is why it is helpful to gather stories before you succinctly define the challenge. The stories provide you with subjective (yes, *subjective*) distance.

When you clearly name a challenge you are offering a gift for the faith community. By doing so, you are encouraging clarity about goals. Maybe the faith community does need a better Sunday School, but to what end? Perhaps the challenge for the congregation is to let go of the unrealistic expectation that religious education is going to expand with just a few changes. Or, maybe the appropriate challenge isn't about drawing more children to education. Maybe it is about paying attention to the children that are already present, hungry for connection with something beyond a mechanized world. Without clarity of purpose, the congregation will be distracted by lesser goals. The many possible goals, spoken or unspoken, that exist are why it is important to correctly and clearly name the challenge. It is your opportunity—and your responsibility—as a leader to clarify and simplify that which is complex.

AN EVOCATIVE ALTERNATIVE

Rev. Teri Thomas at Northminster posed the challenge as a question. *Sunday School has died. Can we bury it and see what might rise from the ashes?*

An alternative to stating your challenge in the form of a concise statement is to offer a brief, evocative question. An evocative question is a powerful expression of the challenge part of the learning journey. It can be used instead of, or with, a succinct statement.

Note how specific Rev. Thomas's question is. There is reference to a specific subject: Sunday School. So, the challenge is about something specific, not a general feeling like "care," or "hope," or "grace." It involves action. The question is crisp, even blunt. It is not rambling with multiple subjects. It is compact. *Can we bury it?* The language is not neutral. The language is evocative in that the words provoke an emotional response and suggest an action. The question invites a response from the listener. The verbs are theological. They are existential. *Died. Bury. See. Rise.* The question invites further consideration. The solution to the problem raised by the question is not something for which leaders can provide training. The congregation will need to lean into the challenge to see what education or even transformation can take place.

Stating your challenge in the form of an evocative question has the effect of focusing emotional discomfort. I do not say lightly that Mr. Rogers speaks the truth when he says, "Anything that is human is mentionable and anything that's mentionable can be more manageable"[5] Such language brings strong images, memories, or feelings to mind. Such language also gives you as a leader something with which to work. You now have people's attention.

That's what Pastor Martin Wright has experienced at the Ogilville Christian Church in Indiana. The congregation started in 1887. Back then, the building was in the middle of nowhere. Nearby was a hitching post and a general store.

Geographically speaking, not much was different when Pastor Wright arrived than when the congregation began. The people still gathered in a rural setting. The building was located at the bend in the road just as it had been more than a century ago. However, now attendance was down to ninety people a week. Pastor Wright was the sixth pastor in a line of several short tenures and quick departures. He felt God's call to move the congregation ahead.

Though it may have been unstated, the congregational culture was holding a question for him: "How are you going to take us back to the good old days?" Asking a question about reclaiming the good old days wasn't going to extend the congregation's pilgrimage in a meaningful way. So, Pastor Wright posed an evocative question: "Are our best days behind us?"

In the years since Pastor Wright's arrival, the Ogilville congregation has thrived in many ways. Attendance has increased well into the three hundreds. The past is honored *and* there are new families that have no connection to the good old days. The one-room church house has been expanded, including creative use of the basement. So, now, several years into his pastorate, Pastor Wright offers his congregation another evocative question, "Does it matter that we're worshiping 370 a week but still have neighbors that we aren't ministering to?"

Pastor Wright's questions are evocative because they are future oriented. They are open-ended. That is, he doesn't answer his question. He is openly and honestly offering the question to others. His questions encourage responses at both the cognitive and emotional level. Such evocative questions encourage specific responses, not generalities.

Clearly describing a challenge with an evocative question or a succinct statement is often the first step in learning how to do something new. Even when it isn't a first part of the journey, there is evidence that a clear and evocative expression of the challenge is how the learning begins.

FUNDAMENTAL BEHAVIORS

Much of this chapter has been devoted to how you will describe the challenge to others. The following sections describe how several of the fundamental behaviors can support your congregation through the process.

Listening for the challenge as it comes up in everyday conversation, eliciting a descriptive story, constructing an evocative question, or creating a succinct statement all occur through the exchange of ideas through spoken word. Such work involves *the art of conversation.*

In addition to constructing stories, an evocative question, or a succinct statement, how and when you share such words are strategic considerations. They are also artful considerations. How and when you share such words is an artful consideration because it involves craft—sharing the challenge with others so that the challenge gets the consideration it deserves. This involves cultivating the ability to bring the challenge up in conversation in a way that does not draw attention to yourself, but to the challenge. It can't be about you.

There is also is artistry involved in communicating a well-crafted challenge. The challenge shouldn't come off sounding like a poorly constructed greeting card sentiment. Pay attention to what words you choose. The impact of Pastor Wright's using the phrase "best days" was a powerful and artful alternative to "good old days."

One common theme in achieving artfulness in talking about the challenge is the leader's commitment to bring up the evocative question or succinct statement repeatedly in different settings. The question or statement becomes a mantra. The word *mantra* means the thought behind a speech or action. This is exactly how an evocative question or challenge statement functions. It reveals the thought that supports the endeavor.

Some congregational leaders think of such repeated statements as something akin to a Biblical proverb. Think of the well-known proverbs from scripture: "The fear of the Lord is the beginning of knowledge" (Prov. 1:7a). "Start children off on the way they should go, and even when they are old they will not turn from it" (Prov. 22:6). "Above all else, guard your heart, for everything you do flows from it" (Prov. 4:23). These are wisdom sayings. They are examples of what a wise person will think or do. Many of them are practical. Many of them have to do with common sense. They are repeatable because they fit any number of situations. Think of your description of the challenge as a proverb you are sharing with others.

Repeating the essence of your challenge as a mantra or proverb can be helpful at many points along the learning journey. The repetition signifies that a direction has been agreed upon even if the path is not clear. Recitation by an increasing number of people indicates that the community, not just a few, are at work on something important. Because of this, you should ask other leaders to be ready to repeat the question or statement that best describes the challenge.

Pastors report that they become understandably flustered when confronted to explain a new undertaking. ("Just why are we going to all the trouble and expense of hiring an architect?") Because the request to explain often comes at inopportune times—immediately after worship, an e-mail received just before bedtime, on the way out the door to visit someone in the hospital—it helps to have a statement ready to explain the essence of the learning journey. Your challenge statement or evocative question serves that purpose. Keep it in mind. Take it with you wherever you go.

The art of conversation is important throughout the learning journey. It is represented in the endeavor of naming the challenge not only through the question or statement that develops, but also in the repetition of the question or statement.

Another important behavior during the challenge phase is discerning to what extent to use an outside resource. When it comes to naming the challenge, the use of an outside resource, while essential to learning, needs to be tentative. Even though an outside resource is the key element of all congregational learning endeavors, not enough is known during the challenge phase of the learning journey to give full energy to one outside resource. Not enough has been decided to go all in with a particular method, practice, or program. One mistake that congregations make is to jump quickly to the answer, to manufacture an inauthentic aha moment.

What does moving to a resource too quickly look like? The minister is addressing the education team of the congregation he serves. He has just stated the challenge they face. It was five minutes ago that he said, "Our children won't sit still for public school–like religious education anymore. We need to engage their whole bodies and minds in order for them to learn about Christ and his Kingdom." Heads nod yes. One person—a public school teacher—says, "Don't sell public education short. It involves far more than sitting at a desk these days." The minister responds a bit sheepishly, "I know you are right, I was just trying to make a point." The teacher says, "I get what you mean. I just hear so many critiques of my vocation these days." There is silence for about five seconds.

Then another member of the group says, "My brother's congregation does something called workshop rotation. It is a great resource. We should do that." The evidence is that workshop rotation is a wonderful resource.[6] And, yes, many congregations use it effectively. However, in this context and at this time, the introduction of the answer is too soon. It is offered to ease discomfort. Not enough learning has taken place. Yet, the team decides to try it anyway. Six months later the congregation is struggling to find volunteers to lead the method. There is nothing in place for September. When someone asks at a meeting, "What's our next step?" the question is met with a group sigh.

Finding the best resource for the context and then adapting that resource with the gifts of the congregational leaders is the most powerful element of a congregation's experience as a learning community. However, moving too fast for an all-encompassing answer while defining the challenge is not a good idea. It is an intervention asserted too soon.

The best outside resources to use while defining a challenge are not lengthy books or expert consultants, but typically short articles about the subject or brief investigative conversations with leaders from other congregations. The goal is to build capacity to look at the learning challenge from a more fulsome perspective. It is not to answer the question. The goal is not to find the solution; the solution has to find you.

Which leads to the connection between *measured pace* and defining the challenge. I have found that congregations tend to move too quickly rather than too slowly when working on a project that requires learning. It is not uncommon for a board to think that defining the challenge is the same as solving the problem. The primary timing question when you have defined the question is not how fast you will solve the challenge, but in what time frame you will test and share the challenge with others.

What is the relationship between defining the challenge and *leadership and learning*? Leadership involves using authority. It involves leveraging influence. If you are a clergyperson, you are the resident theologian for your faith community. You are the witness for tender life stories. Sometimes you are a healer, sometimes a wise sage. In the stories I've collected there is plenty of evidence that clergy (and sometimes lay leaders) are the chief education officers of a congregation. Clergy serve the role of trusted advisor for so many different congregational endeavors. So, while finding the right words for a challenge worth pursuing, there are fundamental questions to keep in mind:

- Is this a challenge your congregation can address?
- Does it fit your congregation?
- Who are your conversation partners so that you are not doing this alone?
- How do you practice your role in simplifying the complicated and clarifying the vague?
- What does this challenge require you to learn?
- Who in the congregation can be your peer learning partners?

Note that all these questions are related to readiness and capacity. These are questions that come to mind because you are thinking about the connection between organizational learning and your congregation's ability to do new things. A primary task of leadership in the challenge phase is to discern if the congregation is prepared to address the passages of the learning journey that will follow.

Think for a moment about the word *curriculum*. After all, a learning journey is like a curriculum. Curriculum isn't the guidebook that tells you how to save Sunday School. Such a guidebook doesn't exist. Curriculum includes the various elements that come together to help your congregation accomplish something new regarding Sunday School. The curriculum includes the planned (formal) and unplanned (informal) experiences that help you learn to do something new. It is your course of study. The etymology for the word *curriculum* refers to running a course or a course of action. Hence, I've called such a passage a "learning journey." Your congregation is running a course, a course of learning.

The course of action you take to address your challenge is a learning journey whether that's what you've been calling it or not. Wise educators avoid creating curricula for learners who are not equipped to learn the subject matter. It does no one good to ask a community to meet a demand of reality for which they are ill-equipped.

For now, celebrate the pursuit and then achievement of the clear description of the challenge ahead of you. It is a significant feat. It will serve you well on the rest of the journey to effectively accomplish something new and important in your congregation. Now that you have a sense of what is at stake, you and other leaders can begin to explore possibilities for action. It is to this *exploration* that we now turn.

You know you are experiencing the challenge phase of a learning journey when the following occur:

- You experience unease about something important to the life of your congregation.
- You aren't sure what the unease is all about.
- You realize the challenge isn't clearly defined.
- The challenge appears over time in different ways or in different experiences.
- The discomfort of avoiding the challenge is stronger than the discomfort of taking on the challenge.
- The stories people are telling about the challenge are more than complaints; they are three-dimensional expressions of your life together.

Questions to ask when you are aware of an emerging challenge include the following:

- Is this something that warrants extensive time and energy?
- What strengths does the congregation already have regarding this challenge?
- What themes appear in the stories about this challenge?
- What have we tried previously regarding this challenge? What worked? What didn't work?
- What outside resource connects well with our capacity and creativity at this moment?

Things you can do when in the midst of defining a challenge include the following:

- Elicit stories about the challenge.
- Develop a succinct statement or question about the challenge that orients others to the learning that needs to take place. The form is this: "We seek to learn . . . in order to (so that) . . ."
- Test iterations of the question or statement of question with a small but diverse audience and seek feedback.
- Revise your orienting statement or question as new information or experiences develop.
- Expand the number of people you are talking to about this challenge at a strategic and judicious pace.
- Celebrate the identification of a challenge as an accomplishment itself.

Chapter Four

Exploration

Searching for Solutions

Exploration is the discernment passage of the learning journey. Exploration involves a pursuit to find a resolution to the challenge. You are on a search. While searching, you scan the environment for clues and cues that will eventually lead to a discovery. But for now, you are on a treasure hunt. Fundamental behaviors that assist this search include finding the right, measured pace for the work, the art of conversation, and thinking of leadership in terms of clergy and laity learning together. It is a time to test outside resources in relationship to your congregation's ingenuity.

A congregation hosts a summer experience for children. The learning experience is about the exodus. The children reenact the escape from Egypt. They are led outdoors to a large field. Once in the large field they receive special eyeglasses. These aren't 3-D glasses. These glasses have a scene fixed on the lenses. When a child looks through the glasses he or she sees another landscape transposed over what is actually there. What the children see is not a Midwestern tree-lined field, but a desert. They see sand. They see mountains in the distance. They see a hazy sun. The children are instructed to look at the scene in silence for thirty seconds. Then they are asked, "What do you notice?" Exploration is about seeing the landscape around you. More than that, it is about noticing, comprehending what you see.

When a congregation takes on a new challenge it is like embarking on an exodus. The dangers may not be as harrowing as the Egyptian army, the rushing Red Sea, or lack of food under an angry sun, but worthwhile challenges do lead a congregation to scan the landscape wondering, "What do we see?"

This phase of the learning journey is called "exploration." Usually exploration is the second passage in the learning journey. Exploration involves a search to find a solution to the challenge. The search is a time of critical reflection about the challenge. It is a time of active learning. It is a time when you will be exploring your environment. You are searching to find a solution to your challenge. You are looking for helpers. You are looking for those with whom to share leadership. You are trying to determine when the time is right to make the next move.

Think of exploration as a quest. It is your congregation's exodus. This time of exploration can indeed feel like forty years, let alone forty days and forty nights. It is the natural inclination of any community, once a challenge is identified, to unscramble the challenge as quickly as possible in order to make the discomfort go away and reap the benefits of the solution. But these things take time. In a true learning journey, you are not just starting a new program, you are creating something that will contribute to a better life together.

Remember that if the challenge is one that keeps the congregation essentially the same, then a learning journey involving exploration is not necessary. However, if the challenge is one that requires changing the essence of the congregation, its purpose, how it sees itself, or how it uses resources, then exploration can hardly be avoided.

When a faith community enters into exploration, it is like a person discerning about a life issue. We do this all the time whether we are conscious of it or not. It is part of decision making related to matters that mean the most to us. Should I take a new job? How do I make changes in my marriage? Do I give more money away this year, and if so, to which organizations?

In the setting of a learning journey, exploration is the process by which your congregation learns to do something new. It involves realization of the absence of capacity. The absence of capacity leads the faith community to search for a new way of looking at the challenge. The search leads to greater ability to act effectively.

Recall St. Timothy's Episcopal Church. Rev. Nickel and lay leaders went on an exploration. They knew they wanted to make their congregation a true sanctuary for young children (and their parents). By defining their challenge, they knew the journey involved more than teaching discipline. This was a faith-formation challenge. So, the exploration moved from focusing on parenting and discipline to scanning the environment for different ways to teach scripture and the ways of worship to the children. They looked for resources to lift their capacity.

Here is another example. The council of a congregation was reviewing their annual statistics. One council member noted that the average age of their congregation was sixty-eight. She said, "I guess we aren't getting any younger."

This led to a longer conversation about who and what God was calling the congregation to be. One person stated, "We need more young adults, that's our challenge." So, for a season the council talked about ways for the congregation to take on a more significant role of mentoring young adults. For some, this conversation was frustrating. There was much talk about young adults. Yet, no one was actually talking *with* young adults.

It was during Lent that the conversation changed. The council was meeting the week after Ash Wednesday. The pastor said, "When I was placing ashes on your foreheads it dawned on me that we should be addressing the spiritual concerns of older adults. That's who God has given us!" So, the council framed a new challenge. They set out to nurture deep relationships with older adults so that faith development continued throughout one's lifespan.

The leaders knew instinctively that they needed to explore what this challenge meant. They didn't have a map for their learning journey. Yet they began to search outside—that is, they talked to outside resources. They learned that the director of the local senior citizens center was a valuable conversation partner. They read a chapter from a book by Jane Marie Thibault and Robert Morgan titled *Pilgrimage into the Last Third of Life: 7 Gateways to Spiritual Growth.*[1]

One person started writing a grant to fund an elevator for greater accessibility. But the council thought things were moving too fast and they asked the person to stop the grant process. Later, the pastor would observe, "Something might be a good idea but the time isn't right." Considerations related to timing are part of exploration.

During this season of exploration, the pastor said he preached a sermon on Abraham and Sarah. "I don't know if I was conscious of it at the time," he would later say, "but we were going through our own late-stage birth experience regarding older adults." The congregation needed to explore various conditions and factors before discovering the best way forward.

When congregations are in the exploration phase, it is important to pay attention to four fundamental behaviors: using outside resources, pace, leadership and learning, and the art of conversation. These fundamental behaviors help congregations observe the landscape accurately. These markers help the congregation to stay on track. They also help the congregation increase its aptitude concerning the challenge. Let's look more closely at these four behaviors as assets for exploration, beginning with outside resources.

USING OUTSIDE RESOURCES

As stated in earlier chapters, combining the use of an outside resource with your creativity is the essential behavior for a learning journey. During your exploration you are likely to consider more resources than at any other time during your journey. It is as if you are preparing for your own exodus to a new land and you are placing essential supplies in your backpack.

A congregational council exploring a sanctuary renovation read a book on building projects. They talked to an architect. They visited another church that had recently made major changes to their worship space. They talked to a professor of worship at a local seminary. No one resource provided the council with a transfiguring moment of clarity concerning the way ahead. Yet each encounter shaped new possibilities about what changes to make to the sanctuary.

The reason no one resource is going to be satisfactory has to with the development aspect of being a learning congregation. It is helpful to assess your congregation's developmental domain during the exploration experience of a learning journey. Are you prepared for training? Or do you need to first do some information gathering? During a successful learning journey you and your colleagues will find that the resources you draw on will reflect the increase in your capacity. Is the congregation ready to have something new drawn from its creativity? If the answer to this question is "yes," then you are ready for resources that will provide you with education, not just training. You could start with a short article, a blog to provide you with information. You might end up working with a coach who might well lead you to a desired transformation.

The assessment of your congregation's developmental stage includes ascertaining the clarity with which the challenge is described, how many and who are involved in the conversation, alignment with mission, consistency with values or a religious worldview, and what your congregation actually does with a resource when you engage it.

Finding the best resources for your challenge helps you do the right thing in the right way.[2] A lay leader is describing her congregation's challenge: "We want to start a weekday program for children so that young people who don't go to church can be introduced to our faith." She said that first her team did Internet searches about afterschool activities sponsored by congregations. This gave them needed information.

Soon the team was ready for training. They still weren't sure what the new program would be like, but a nearby church was hosting a one-day workshop on children, the arts, and faith. A team of five attended. From this event they learned about arts. Even more helpful was the information they gained about operational aspects of hosting a children's afterschool experience—securing registrations, sending out invitations, getting background checks for leaders, and so forth.

During a council meeting a member said, "I'm all for an afterschool program, but is art what we are about?" This led the team to secure a facilitator to help them talk through the issue of mission alignment, to identify congregational assets and community needs. Now, the congregation had moved from seeking information and training, to becoming educated about the challenge. A true exploration was taking place.

Though the path ahead still needed more clearing, the congregation was learning the right way to do the right thing.

TIME AND A MEASURED PACE

Was it the philosopher Aristotle who wrote that a person with excellent character did the right thing in the right way at the right *time*? This is called "practical wisdom."[3] Doing the right thing is important. Doing the right thing well leads to effective outcomes. Additionally, knowing how to read time is part of practical wisdom. Learning from a period of exploration involves a sense of good timing.

Sometimes the element of timing involves knowing whether or not to take on a specific project now. A congregation's board had long wanted to plant a new church across town. The board dreamed of this new community of faith. An external assessment tool was used to help the leaders determine exactly where the new congregation should be located. However, a pastor who was new to the congregation gathered a small group and for three months explored the challenge in terms of finances, mission alignment, and long-term capacity. He soon reported to the rest of the board, "Not now, not in this season, not yet." This turned out to be a true discernment. The result was new energy placed toward an English-as-a-second-language teaching program that took place within their existing building. The board had a wonderful dream. They were exploring options in the right way. However, the time wasn't right.

Sometimes timing and exploration go together on a micro scale. This can be as specific as knowing the right time to have a conversation with another person. Or it can be as nuanced as knowing *when* to bring in an outside resource. If you do it too soon, you will be giving away some of your own agency. If too late, it may be more difficult to remedy one of the inevitable mistakes that happen along the way.

Timing is difficult to get right. It is likely that at first your congregation will either move too quickly or too slowly. Typically, a congregation is not predisposed one way or another. It is always in relation to the challenge. For example, one large nondenominational congregation knew they needed more staff to accomplish their mission. So, the board gave the senior pastor the power to make hiring decisions for four months. The leaders felt a sense of urgency. They reasoned that this was the time to be aggressive. And being aggressive in hiring meant that one person needed flexibility to make quick decisions. Unfortunately, the value of speed outdistanced the values of the right thing in the right way. Soon, the congregation was spending too much money on staff, facing a deficit, and dealing with staff conflicts that had not existed before. Moving fast did not produce a positive result.

This congregation's sense of timing was not productive in relationship to the staffing issue. At about the same time, the same congregation was trying to decide whether or not to establish a covenant relationship with a village in Kenya. Clearly, and early on, everyone wanted to do this. One leader asked, "What's keeping us from doing this now?" The response back was, "We don't know what *this* is." So the leaders slowed down. They explored various aspects of a covenant relationship. What is our goal? Who will be involved? What will this cost? Why are we doing this? What will success look like? Three years after the "What's keeping us from doing this now?" question was asked, fifteen people from the congregation were hosting guests from Kenya in their homes for the first time—evidence that slowing down previously was the right thing to do. Slowing down at one moment in time helped produce wonderful results later.

What else does a measured pace look like? It is as much a way of thinking about exploration as it is a literal timeline. Thus slowing down may take many forms. It might be as subtle as slowing the pace of a conversation so that questions can be asked and answers can be explored. Slowing down might be as evident as lengthening the process in order to explore the religious framework of a potential new approach.

Decelerating the strategic thinking of a congregation is a way to counter the predictable rush to judgment that many groups experience while making decisions. Such haste is rarely because a quick decision is absolutely necessary. The haste more likely reflects the leaders' need to be less anxious. If the problem is solved or the decision is made, then the leaders don't have to worry about it anymore. Although quick decisions often lower the immediate anxiety of the congregation, they also often sacrifice long-term results and produce larger, enduring concerns.

Lowering discomfort is not a good enough reason to act urgently, particularly if there is no crisis. Of course, some issues in congregations need prompt attention. However, when it comes to strategic endeavors, slowing the pace leads to wiser judgments that have stronger results. Congregational life has many emotional dynamics that do not contribute to clear thinking. Excellent strategy requires clear thinking, and that requires time. Slowing down allows careful thinking to regulate anxiety. It also is about more than feelings. Slowing down helps a congregation's thinking catch up with its praying and its praying to catch up with its thinking.

One congregation experienced slowing down as a virtue. This congregation wanted to share their building with another congregation or not-for-profit organization. Why? They sought an additional income stream for their budget. The building is in a good downtown location and the likelihood was that there would be several options. They were ready to move ahead with a decision—the budget deadline was looming—when someone said, "Hey, shouldn't we be thinking about what kind of match best serves our mission?" That question slowed the process.

Slowing the process sharpened their thinking. They sought counsel from other congregations who share their buildings. They found a document on-line that described several positives and negatives of sharing a facility. The committee consulted with an attorney about rental contracts. They began thinking about the long-term mission of the congregation and its use of space. It has taken longer to find a building partner (the budget process survived the delay). However, the exploration space is widening and the leaders have sharper clarity about their congregation's mission.

So, how can you tell if you are moving too fast? Impact will be limited. Conflict will occur. As a leader you will feel regret or anger (depending on your temperament). The primary sign that you are moving too fast while you are in the midst of an endeavor is that your pace results in avoiding or resisting something you should be doing instead. Are you avoiding a difficult conversation, not asking a hard question, not looking at negative realities, or not learning a necessary skill?

Though it is less likely, this is what exploring too slowly looks like: The circle of people involved is not increasing. No one has described what success might look like. There is not a shared sense of the next steps (or there is a shared sense and no one has come forward to do them). Enthusiasm is fading. The attention span of those involved wanes. There is resentment: "Am I the only one working on this?"

Though more congregations move too quickly rather than too slowly, you will want to observe signs of avoidance. If you find a work group talking about the same issue meeting after meeting, then it is likely that the group is avoiding some aspect of the challenge. Some congregations procrastinate while exploring a certain challenge. In such situations, leaders will feel as if they never have enough data. Leaders will feel as if there is always more to explore. The person who says, "I think we finally have enough information. We know the right thing to do" will be offering a gift to the congregation.

The Hebrew word for day is *yom*. "God called the light Day, and the darkness he called Night. And there was evening and there was morning, the first day" (Gen. 1:5). The word *yom* denotes a day not necessarily as humanity understands it, but a day in God's time. It is not necessarily an orderly day but the Day of God. It contains the practical stuff of life tracked by the luminous long clock of the Creator. Time is a moment of undetermined length in which something special is unfolding. God's time is measured in relationship to the intuitive sense of the right thing.

Special things are unfolding in your congregation. Your congregation is the steward of the best claims and commitments of your faith—over the long haul. Such claims and commitments are worthy of your extended attention. Take a breath. Slow down. Pay attention. Think carefully. Explore. These things take time.

LEADERSHIP AND LEARNING

When your congregation explores how to address something new, a key element to effectiveness is the relationship between leadership and learning. There are many things to say about leadership. There are many things to say about learning. For your congregation to gain new skills, consider the synchronization of leadership *and* learning.

My friend Dr. James Rafferty says, "Leadership is the activity of helping people get to where they would go if they only knew how." Leadership often denotes a guide, the act of directing a course or a direction. When combined with learning, leadership signifies a person who helps an individual or a group *learn* a new course or direction. Leadership and learning together denote relationships where new capacities are learned.

Inspiration often needs deeper consideration. A pastor states boldly that she wants her church to open up the only homeless shelter in town. Others in the congregation bless this idea. However, no one really knows how to accomplish this. Does the congregation have the funds? No. Has the congregation trained people how to be volunteers at a homeless shelter? Not yet. Is there clarity about the goals? The answer is, "We're working on it." Leadership and learning go together in the growing capacity of the congregation to take on the new mission, to view the exploration of the challenge as a new course of study. The process of people in the congregation learning together will lead them to accomplish something that was previously only wishful thinking.

So, exploration about a congregational challenge not only requires careful attention to timing but also attention to the coordination of leadership and learning. Such coordination highlights the nature of the relationship between clergy and laity.

BLEST BE TIES THAT BIND

Pastor Marty Wright knew something had to be different. (We met Marty in the previous chapter.) The Ogilville Christian Church that invited him to be pastor had been through a rough time. Attendance was dropping. Too many pastors had come and gone. The good work that could be done in the small town was lost in long business meetings. The building needed much attention. It was overwhelming at first.

Marty had never served a congregation as senior pastor. So, the challenge of this new endeavor had him thinking. And praying. "What can I do to set a new tone?" It is hard for a congregation to go through a series of clergy leaders in a short period of time. The quick procession of prior clergy leaders left little room for positive attachments to develop. Yes, he knew that it is a spiritual mistake to confuse the pastoral leader with the person of God. Yet, the pastoral leader is the steward of the mission and vision of the faith community. A healthy congregation needs a trusted leader.

Congregants naturally project expectations upon clergy leaders. Sometimes the projections can be helpful; sometimes projected expectations are not helpful. Some congregants idealize the role of the pastor feeling that the pastor is closer to the sacred. In such situations there is an expectation that the clergy should know the solution to every challenge. This type of projection hampers exploration.

For difficult endeavors in life it is understandable that we want answers. We seek solutions. So, sometimes we project these desires upon clergy (and parents, politicians, teachers, and others with formal authority). Sometimes clergy are understandably tempted to affirm this projection. After all, it can be validating to be seen as one who knows.

Have you read the poem by William Stafford titled "A Ritual to Read to Each Other"? It begins:

> If you don't know the kind of person I am
> and I don't know the kind of person you are
> a pattern that others made may prevail in the world
> and following the wrong god home we may miss our
>   star.[4]

Maladaptive projections reside in us and through our relationships. They are certainly present when congregations explore challenges. It is so easy (and tempting) to create patterns that may prevail in the world—patterns that hinder our exploration. If the pattern is pervasive enough, then we may indeed miss our star.

Missing our star is the equivalent of not living up to our God-graced potential. It may be represented by broken relationships. Missing our star might be represented by the congregation's failing to live up to what God intends. If the pattern is disruptive enough some characters get stuck repeating the same hurtful patterns. ("We've never been able to resolve our conflicts!") Thus, the roadmap of exploration may look like a constellation with missing lights. Following the wrong god home corresponds to taking on the wrong challenges or not trusting God's timing—not seeing new tasks as learning opportunities.

In many congregations there are healthy attachments between the clergy and members. Hope and trust become forecasts formed from a base of positive early interactions. Learning congregations are made up of people who know how to make relationships work. In such congregations people find they can depend on one another. A healthy balance between authority and collaboration exists in the congregation. People feel safe. After all, when a congregation is led to go where it would if it only knew how, there is almost always a pattern of highly healthy relationships between clergy and laity.

So, yes, Marty Wright pursued deep discernment. He prayed. He wanted this pastoral relationship to be different. He prayed more. He prayed even more. The answer to his prayers came in the form of towel and basin. Jesus's actions as described in John's Gospel entered his mind and wouldn't leave. "He poured water into a basin and began to wash the disciples' feet and to wipe them with the towel that was tied around him" (John 13:5). Marty had never participated in a foot washing ritual before, it wasn't a practice rooted in his religious tradition. This was something the Eastern Orthodox do, not rural evangelicals. Yet, in these first days of ministry at this congregation that was ready to move ahead if it only knew how, Marty welcomed the elders with a basin full of water and plenty of clean cloths. "I knew I had to do this," Marty remembers, "We had to form a team of mutual servants and we needed to do it from the start."

Marty also remembers, perhaps not fear, but something more than hesitation. *This could break my ministry before it even starts: a stranger with a new, foreign ritual.*

As the shoes came off and the water was splashed ever so carefully, humility replaced any fear or hesitation. The sense of healthy humility that filled the room was contagious. It was a behavior, a ritual, to offer one another as a visual representation of service. For this congregation a different image was developing about what it meant to be clergy and laity, together, leading a congregation.

Books and articles describing effective congregation life emphasize the importance of clergy leadership. There are many clergy leadership models that, each in their own way, are described as important to the health of a congregation. There are many tools and techniques clergy use to be effective, not only as pastors, but also as managers and leaders. Depending on one's tradition, these models, tools, and techniques are known as servant leadership, Christ-like leadership, self-differentiation, emotional intelligence, adaptive leadership, transformational leadership, and so on. Many of these models, tools, and techniques are helpful. They make a difference in terms of the maturity of clergy and how they lead.

Of course, laity involvement is also lifted up as key to congregational health. The work of the congregation is not solely the responsibility of clergy. So, congregations work on helping laity identify their gifts or find their niche. Some congregations make sure that laity go through thorough training.

Clearly, lay preparation and proper leadership skills for clergy are important parts of congregational development. However, more important than preparation and skills is the *relationship* between clergy and laity. Congregations that effectively explore their challenges experience clergy and laity who learn together about the things that matter most to the congregation. Learning together creates the opportunity for a distinctive relationship between clergy and laity.

In the best situations, the relationship between clergy and lay leaders is characterized by a kind of *affection* that is unique—different from other relationships. It includes respect, but it is more than respect. It is more than the honoring of office and roles. This affection includes friendship but it is a kind of friendship. It is not necessarily shaped by the sharing of intimacies— that is, the sharing of deep secrets and wounds. This friendship is characterized by closeness that comes not so much from sharing vulnerabilities as it comes from sharing a common purpose. The affection that is noticeable between clergy and lay leaders in congregations that accomplish what they set out to do is exemplified by competence and character in the pursuit of common, God-focused goals. This dynamic is what brings a lay leader to tell her friend, "We just love our pastor." This affection is what leads the clergyperson to look out from the place she stands to preach and think, "I love these people." And it is one of the primary conditions that helps a congregation learn how to accomplish new things.

At its best the clergy and laity learning relationship demonstrates many positive traits, including something peculiarly like affection. It is the relationship between mutual learners. Think back to the healthiest relationships you had in school. How would you describe the nature of the give and take between schoolmates, whether in elementary school, high school, or college? There is, for many of us, a palpable affection that occurs in the relationships we have with schoolmates. (After all, why are reunions both so dreaded and popular?) Furthermore, many of us remember a class in school, not just because of the subject, but because of our positive relationship with the teacher. We may have liked the subject. We loved the teacher. That is, we had an appropriate affection for the teacher because of his or her warmth and interest in our development.

It is this kind of affection that occurs when clergy and laity learn together about the things that matter most to them.

Such warmth is preached in Romans 12 and is framed by language about learning. Early in the chapter the exhortation is for the faithful to be "transformed by the renewing of your minds." There is a description of different gifts, including teaching. In verse 10 it reads, "love one another with mutual affection; outdo one another in showing honor" (Rom. 12:10). The Greek for mutual affection is *philostorgos*—to be devoted to, to be kindly affectionate toward, tenderly loving.

Congregations where clergy and laity learn together about the things that matter most to them in an atmosphere of *philostorgos* are well equipped to address the challenges and opportunities they face.

The Rev. Anastassia Zinke has experienced *philostorgos*. She is the clergy leader at All Souls Unitarian Church. Not too long ago Anastassia was the *new* clergy leader at All Souls. There are so many things to explore when you are the new clergy leader. As one who, initially, stands at the threshold of the congregation, you see so many things that should or could be done. For Anastassia every conversation was like mirror talk. She was imagining that laity were holding up mirrors so that she could see herself. And Anastassia was holding a mirror up to the laity so they could see themselves.

Soon, this became overwhelming. I don't know about you but I can only look at myself in the mirror for so long. It is very uncomfortable. This is what Anastassia felt. So, she said, "I put the mirrors away." To learn about this congregation, to explore its possibilities she said, "I would—we would—simply see each other."

One of the first things she did was to leave the pulpit to preach. Her preaching changed. It became more conversational. It was easier to pick up nonverbal signals from parishioners. The content flowed more naturally. Just as interesting to Anastassia was how people's connection with her changed. Before a person might say, after a sermon, "Nice job." Or another might come up to her and say, "Oh, I was thinking about the . . . oh, never mind." With the change, many for the first time offered their own kind of blessing to her after the sermon in the form of a hug. During the week she started receiving e-mails following up on the subject of the sermon. "Oh, never minds," were replaced with honest, searching conversation. The sermon became an occasion for connection. The affection was real. She was no longer seeing projections when she interacted with laity. At All Souls, clergy and laity were looking directly at one another and liking what they saw.

If you are a pastor, it may not be washing the feet or preaching without a manuscript that leads you into a vital relationship with your congregation. You will have to find your own way. Whatever way you find, know that exploring new things for your congregation is quickened by the affection between clergy and laity.

In the movie *Before Sunrise*, two people who have just met each other are talking about what matters most to them. One of them, Jesse, is saying that he'd rather accomplish something important in life than to have "only been in a really nice, caring relationship."[5] Celine disagrees. She says,

> I really believe that if there's any kind of God, he wouldn't be in any one of us—not you, not me—but just this space in between. If there's some magic in this world, it must be in the attempt of understanding someone else, sharing something, even if it's almost impossible to succeed. But who cares—the answer must be in the attempt.[6]

When congregations learn to do new things, clergy and laity experience some kind of magic, the abiding presence of God in the space between people and in the space between people and the subject at hand.

Such space is not empty space. It holds affection. It holds meaning. Such space is filled with *philostorgos*.

Remember Pastor Marty Wright referenced earlier in this chapter? Marty remembers one Sunday. He had been at the congregation for about seven years. Things were going well. It was a hard-earned kind of well. He and his elders had mutually worked on communication, vision, shared values, and how they treated each other. They had learned to be a governing council, together.

On this Sunday, he moved away from the pulpit, down among the pews. He could see the eyes of not only his elders but also of all others in the congregation. He preached without notes, "It's true, I have come not only to know you, but to love you. I love this congregation. I love who you are as people. And I appreciate the affection you have for me. Thank you. Thanks be to God."

EXPLORATION AND THE ART OF CONVERSATION

Paying attention to timing and honoring relationships between clergy and laity helps you explore your challenge more deeply. No matter your challenge, you periodically need to discern whether the challenge you've identified is the right one. You need to resurvey the landscape of possibilities. You will want to run small experiments to see if you are headed in the best direction. All this takes place without a full epiphany. That probably won't come until later.

Have you set the congregation's sights on the right thing? No wonder moving slowly is often a virtue. Before you act you are stepping back to make sure you are going in the right direction. No wonder relationships matter so much. Before the definite way forward comes your way, you need to foster flourishing relationships.

What are other considerations of exploration? Attention to the art of conversation continues to be important. Specifically, congregations report that exploration is an ideal time to be asking open-ended questions. Parker Palmer writes, "An *open* question is one that expands rather than restricts your arena of exploration, one that does not push or even nudge you toward a particular way of framing a situation."[7] An open question is one that you do not know the answer to.

Asking open-ended questions while exploring a new congregational possibility is very different from deciding on a challenge and then moving immediately to action. The great wide open of not knowing quite what to do is an essential phase along the journey.

Remember the congregation that was exploring older adult ministry after the pastor's Ash Wednesday revelation? Here are some examples of open-ended questions that fit their situation:

What are the primary concerns of older adults in our community?

How does one's relationship with God change through the years?

What is one thing that an older adult does not need or want from a congregation?

What is one gift that you (directed to an older adult) dearly want to share with another?

There are answers to these questions. But the answers are unique depending on to whom the question is directed. It would be difficult to anticipate any individual's response. A collection of answers will provide valuable information for further discernment. Exploration through such questions will reveal possibilities.

As a leader you are going to need to help others with this aspect of the art of conversation. For many of us it is difficult to frame open-ended questions. We can't help ourselves. Our questions just come out with the answer embedded within. Again, think of the congregation considering new ways to engage older adults. Here are well-meaning questions, but they are not open-ended.

Is one of your major concerns as an older adult your finances?

Aren't you closer to God the longer you live?

Do you want more or need more attention from the pastor?

Is your primary gift to offer wisdom?

An open-ended question rarely can be answered with a "yes" or a "no." They are an invitation to ponder. Such questions give control of the answer to the receiver. They elicit feelings. They elicit stories. You are not seeking facts. You are looking for the person to share something important to him or her that you cannot guess.

You might be thinking that this is a lot of work to launch a new program in your congregation. Remember though that this is more than launching a new program. This is about accomplishing something new that is consistent with who God is calling you to be as a community. This is about time. And it is about relationships. Ultimately it is about the embodiment of faith. And the life of faith is made up of many blessed questions that are revealed over time.

God wants Moses to challenge the oppressive ways of Pharaoh. Moses says to God, "If I come to the Israelites and say to them, 'The God of your ancestors has sent me to you,' and they ask me, 'What is his name?' what shall I say to them?" (Exod. 3:13).

This is an essential, open-ended question. It also marked the beginning of a very long yet essential exploration called the "Exodus" for the Israelites.

Or, Jesus of Nazareth gets ready to tell the parable of the mustard seed. He doesn't just jump in. He provides a prologue, which is in the form of a question: "With what can we compare the kingdom of God, or what parable will we use for it?" (Mark 4:30–32).

Questions in scripture move the action forward. Questions in scripture create curiosity. Such questions create tension. The tension is often only resolved by deeper reflection.

Exploring new things in your congregation isn't about finding the right answer quickly (or all by yourself). It is about learning to ask better questions in relationship with those you care about.

Even with the most effective passage of exploration there are going to be setbacks. Learning is seldom linear; learning is hardly ever straight and narrow. We are easily disenchanted. Disappointment is common, if not preordained. Best be ready for it. Readiness for disappointment along the learning journey is the subject of the next chapter.

You know you are experiencing the exploration phase of a learning journey when the following occur:

- You find yourself searching for an answer even if you don't know what the answer would look like or sound like.
- A pastor spends more time with laity because they are working on a defined challenge.
- You feel close to those with whom you are working.
- You are wondering when the right time is to let more people know about the challenge.
- You are looking for the right outside resource.
- You are wondering if you are in over your head.
- You are talking to other congregations about what you want to do.
- You are getting more clarity about what you most need to learn.
- You see that the challenge is larger than you originally thought.
- You are wondering if God is going to offer you an epiphany.

Questions to ask when you are moving through the experience of exploration include the following:

- What resources have been most helpful so far?
- Do your leaders learn best as a learning community by reading, listening, experiencing? How does the answer shape how you will learn together from a resource?
- Who do you really want to talk to but haven't yet approached?
- If you wanted to talk to someone outside the congregational world, who would it be?
- How are you going to adapt what you learn from a resource so it fits your context?
- How is your timing? What would a measured pace look like?

Things you can do when in the midst of exploration include the following:

- Pay attention to relationships. Work on building mutual affection between clergy and laity.
- Name the conditions and factors at work regarding the challenge as it is presently defined.
- Pay attention to time.
- Ask lots of open-ended questions.
- Keep looking for the best resource fit.

Chapter Five

Disappointment

Learning from Inevitable Setbacks

Congregations aren't magically protected from *disappointment*. All kinds of good projects grind to a halt. When this happens, you can't help but feel disappointed. Natural and inevitable feeling of sadness arrive. That is the way of disillusionment. Almost every successful congregational endeavor contains some dissatisfaction. There are ways to address such disappointment. The behavior of practicing *religious coherence* can be helpful; that is, relying on a lucid understanding of faith to lead you back on track.

People have migrated from a land far away. These immigrants have found a worship home at a congregation located in an urban area. The pastor of the congregation, the Rev. Tom Bartley, sees these new relationships as opportunities for friendship. The potential relationships are an opportunity for the congregation to be a missional church. The reality also includes the potential for disappointment.

At first, things go well. Many who have migrated have spent much of their life in refugee camps. If you are like me, you can't imagine the conditions. Running from danger. No privacy. No warmth. Food is limited; daily hygiene constrained. Life is dirty and soiled. I would not do well in such circumstances.

No wonder this population finds their new church as a kind of Canaan. The church is a promised land that has been reached. These are friendly confines. There is warmth; there is food and water. There is space to worship and learn.

The host congregation is more than one hundred years old. Like many congregations, there aren't as many in worship as there used to be. Tom says to his leaders, "If you do what God has called you to do, God will provide you the resources."

Yet, even the best of intentions run the risk of going awry. It isn't easy to share a building. All kinds of logistics need attention. And there is the potential for all kinds of cultural mismatches. How could there not be? Members walk into the kitchen and find food still out on counters. What looks to be a supper lingers cold in open skillets.

As a member of the congregation, you excuse yourself from a committee meeting to go to the rest room. Your first thought when you turn on the light is, "This place needs attention." Trash is littered on the floor. The walls are dirty. This is what happens when more people use the building. You think to yourself: *Remember, our guests have been to hell and maybe not yet all the way back.*

Is this a clash of values? Are expectations too high? Is this what happens when a native congregation befriends an immigrant population? One thing is clear. It is a disappointment. You had hoped that you and others in the congregations could befriend the immigrants. But now operational issues about sharing the building are making it difficult.

What if you are the pastor and your hope has become a fear? That is, you hoped that God would provide. What if God has called your congregation to offer hospitality to refugees and you do not have the resources to achieve what you seek to do?

INEVITABLE DISAPPOINTMENT

No matter how gifted your congregation is at addressing a challenge, you will experience some kind of disappointment along a learning journey. The disappointment may arrive as a feeling of being let down. It may be a feeling of frustration because the endeavor is not going as expected. Disappointment may be the result of something hoped for that did not happen. Congregations working on learning to do something new may experience disappointment as the unfortunate, unintended consequences of progress.

Whatever the cause and effect, disappointment is inevitable somewhere along the learning journey. It most often shows up during the time of exploration. The reality is that disappointment is possible throughout the learning journey.

Any endeavor worth its effort has the potential for disappointment. This is true for congregational endeavors just as it is true for relationships, social causes, and corporate life. It is true for almost any experience of learning whether it is the seventh grader studying hard for a test and then receiving a "C," or an adult trying piano lessons for the first time and finding that playing is not as easy as it looks on YouTube.

Disappointment can be analogous to other experiences. It is akin to ambivalence. It produces feelings of discouragement. Though some good can come from disappointment, disappointment itself is not a good thing. Though one can learn from disappointment, the learning does not offset the negative energy that disappointment prompts. Disappointment involves the realization of limitations. *We had hoped that this project would be the one.*

The particular disappointment that a congregation experiences is shaped by the particular challenge it engages. That is, disappointment isn't a concept. It is embedded in reality. One congregation discovers that it is not going to meet its goal of raising one million dollars for renovations. The thermometer graphic in the narthex is stuck at $790,000. A pastor wants his congregation to study the parables during Lent. It is part of a Biblical literacy effort described in a recent strategic plan. However, only four people register for the class. She had hoped for at least twenty. An urban congregation reaches out to a local school offering tutoring services by its members. The school principal, well meaning but overwhelmed, declines saying this is just one more thing to administrate.

Or, you want to lead a missional church to become friends with strangers from a foreign land and the mess in the bathrooms becomes like a border wall.

Disappointment occurs as an unanticipated barrier to meeting goals. While trying to state clearly what you seek to do you realize that the challenge you thought you were addressing is not the right one for your congregation. During exploration you may realize that there isn't enough positive energy to work the challenge beyond problem definition. Sometimes you wait for an epiphany—a moment of clarity—and it never comes. If only you knew the correct answer you would take the next step. Sometimes the disappointment—let's call it "failure" for a moment—is felt when your congregation is taking on (that is, implementing) the new program and you find that the budget isn't sufficient, or that people only *said* they were interested. You are standing in an empty parking lot wondering where everyone is.

This is true: if you try to accomplish something new in your congregation you will experience disappointment.

EXPECTATIONS

Your congregation may desire more than it can realistically expect to achieve. Particularly in the United States, there is a cultural bias regarding success that leads both individuals and communities to judge themselves against the rare but exceptional public victories of a few. This leads to unrealistic expectations; unrealistic expectations lead to disappointment.

A congregation spent a year designing a playground. They had no kids in worship ("other congregations seem to have so many more children than we do"). The board thought that a playground would attract more youth. Once the playground was built, the congregation stood outside and dedicated it with prayer. Then for *two* years, they waited. No children used the slide. No children raced to the swings. A member asked, "This was supposed to bring us kids. Why did we waste our time?"

The head of the project said, "I guess we are all just disappointed."

Some congregations carry an untested theology of disappointment that is not helpful. Among people of faith there can be a sense that things *should* work out. Hope should always triumph. If things don't work out, this is a sign that something is askew. God is withholding God's favor.

If things don't work out then unconsciously, if not consciously, people could carry the sense that God has judged the congregation negatively. As one pastor said after she called off a mission trip because of lack of funds, "I had a nightmare that consisted of God's finger poking me in the back."

It is disorienting to claim God's affirmation of a project only to have it fail. This doesn't just happen to narcissistic clergy with visions of heavenly grandeur. It happens all the time in neighborhood congregations trying to do simple good.

So, it is best not to theologize about disappointment (or failure) with God as the agent. God is not the actor in the disenchantment of your congregational challenges. God is on the side of congregational development. If things don't work out then it is just that way. The work of God is most evident in your response to the disappointment.

Scripture is full of disappointment. In scripture, disappointment isn't conveyed as a problem, but as a condition. Adam and Eve have to leave Eden. Moses doesn't enter the promised land. Sara goes childless for a long time. Israel is sent to exile. Jesus thwarts people's expectations of the Messiah. *You are not who we were expecting. We had hoped you were the one.* The offering for Jerusalem has mixed results. The early church experiences leadership transition issues. These scriptural experiences represent various disappointments. The frequency of such disappointment normalizes such experiences. Disappointment isn't rare. It is part of life, which means it is also part of congregational life.

LEADING WITH DISAPPOINTMENT

Disappointment in a congregation provides leaders an opportunity to truthfully interpret setbacks. This interpretation occurs at the intersection of leadership and learning. Yes, disappointment is a natural occurrence. It is part of learning and is indeed unsettling. But because the faith community has a whole array of virtues that can be called upon, you and those you lead can come to terms with the sense of letdown without being done in by it. Disappointment can be named. It doesn't need to be reframed. It doesn't need to be denied. There are alternatives.

One alternative is captured in what Craig Dykstra writes: "Faith means freedom, the freedom at last to give up the anxious and impossible task of keeping oneself from falling."[1] A leader who is able to respond to disillusionment with this kind of faith offers a gift to congregants. Congregants are given an example of trust related to congregational life that models a healthy response to the daily disappointments that congregants experience in other aspects of life. Remember that congregational learning involves one of three realms. It involves the operational, the overtly religious, and that of life practice. These realms, of course, overlap. Learning in one helps strengthen learning in the others. Learning not just to fall, but to give up the impossible task of keeping oneself from falling is close to the heart of God. There aren't many life lessons more important. Responding with trust to disappointment provides congregants an experience that applies not just to congregational issues, but also to life itself. In other words, as you help your congregants address congregational disappointment you are modeling for them ways to deal with disappointment in other spheres of life. This is one of the major benefits of viewing your congregation as a learning organization. The learning that takes place in the congregation benefits congregants as they navigate through life challenges including vocation, marriage, education, and so forth.

Another response to disappointment is to *choose your disappointment*. I learned this phrase from Dr. James Rafferty. Choosing one's disappointment is different from resignation. It is not the same as compromise. It is not the same as choosing between the lesser of two evils. Choosing your disappointment means that, given the inevitability of setbacks, a healthy response is to take on an alternate, less-than-perfect path as an intentional decision—not something that has happened to you, but something that you elect. Choosing one's disappointment is a sign that you and your congregation have been able to integrate the positive and negative realities of life. Even Eden had a tree of good and evil.

Of course this does not mean that one opts for tragedy or prefers setbacks. However, regarding life's inevitable regrets (what Freud called "ordinary misery" or "common unhappiness"), the option of choosing your disappointment keeps you as the active agent of your own life.[2] Such a response makes you more than a spectator in relationship to setbacks. In congregational life, it is a learning move to keep the initiative where it belongs: with you and your leaders not with the forces that are pushing back. Absent such initiative, congregational culture becomes passive. People accept negative outcomes as preordained. People think things like "the neighborhood is changing, what can we do?" or "We're a small church, things just work against us." Yet, you and your congregational colleagues are not victims of circumstance. No, choose your disappointment. That is, be a dynamic learner in the midst of the inescapable frustrations that occur in congregational life.

Furthermore, it is best, when possible, to get to the disappointment early. When St. Timothy's Episcopal Church was looking to initiate its new children's ministry, they also explored the possibility of hiring a children's ministry leader. It wasn't too long before they discovered that this was not a viable alternative for them. There were many ways forward, but hiring more staff was not going to be the first step. This was a letdown. But it didn't stop forward movement.

THE PREMORTEM EXERCISE

One way to get to the disappointment early is through an exercise called a "premortem." The premortem was developed by researcher Gary Klein.[3] You can do this exercise with the team that is addressing a particular challenge. It can be done early in any learning journey. It is a preventive intervention. The premortem exercise makes defenses visible. It helps you anticipate potential disappointments and make course corrections. It also, paradoxically, uncovers the hidden expertise of members of the group.

Here is how it works. Let's use St. Timothy's Episcopal as an example. With a group, develop a future story where things have gone terribly awry. Purposely develop a negative scenario. Developing a negative scenario may sound counterintuitive. Yet, bringing potential negative dynamics to the surface is how the learning takes place in this exercise.

So, it is two years after the education team started redeveloping the children's ministry. It has not gone well. There are fewer children learning about God than before. It is impossible to get volunteers. There is no money dedicated to children and their faith formation. Most of the new families with children have left the church. The leader will ask the group, "What went wrong? What contributed to our disappointment?"

Have people write their individual responses down on paper.

Now, have people share them. Post the responses for everyone to see.

Once you have the responses posted, ask participants, "What do you notice?"

Name what went wrong.

Share with the group the observation that it is wise to be aware of what could go wrong. Being aware means the group is more likely to avoid these negative dynamics. Such factors are now in front of the group and not hidden away. The premortem exercise moves the potential pitfalls out of the congregation's blind spot and into plain view. Preventive work can now take place.

Now, ask people to comment on their observations more specifically. Is there a life experience that informs what they shared?

After people share their experiences, note that the various stories represent expertise that will help the congregation succeed rather than be disappointed by that which could go wrong. For example, if someone says, "We aren't able to work well as a team," then note, "I bet you have experience about what good teamwork requires. Let's talk about that." The person now shares what he or she knows about good teamwork. In other words, when individuals share a story about their experience with what could go wrong they are sharing the very expertise that will help the group succeed.

When going on a learning journey it is best to get to the disappointment early. The premortem exercise helps you do that.

RELIGIOUS COHERENCE

The experience of disappointment can lead you to reconsider why you set out on the learning journey in the first place. Disappointment is an invitation to consider the depth of your aspiration. Is this how I want to spend my time? A setback in the midst of a complicated challenge is an opportunity to consider the alignment of your strongest values with the endeavor. Frustration is an opportunity to reflect on why the project was important to you in the first place.

Considering the value of your pursuit is a type of faith reflection. In terms of the learning journey, this is pursuing *religious coherence*—the ability to think clearly about God. Religious coherence leads to action congruent with a religious worldview. Such congruence and coherence strengthens your congregation's ability to take on new challenges. Setbacks are the right occasions to find the words that express how your congregation understands God. There is a positive relationship between the ability of leaders to think and speak lucidly about religious questions and congregational capacity. Rather than experiencing disappointment as forcing you to look down, think of disappointment as an incentive to look up and see if there is a transcendent reason to continue on your journey.

PRESCHOOLS, PARKING LOTS, AND BONHOEFFER

If a congregation is beginning a new preschool, it is necessary to learn how to *do* preschool. That is, it is necessary to learn about staff configuration, curriculum, integration with other ministries, advertising, and any number of things related to starting the best preschool possible. There is the possibility that progress can stop around any one of these issues. The ability to move ahead is assisted if leaders interpret the effort through the religious commitments of the congregation. This means using scripture, theological reflection, raising up faith practices that are consistent with what otherwise might appear to be an operational matter. If it is not possible to frame the effort (and the disappointment) through congregational religious understanding, then that is a sign that perhaps the effort is not worth the time it is being given. Clear articulation of the religious commitment behind an effort contributes to a culture of religious coherence for a faith community. It is crucial behavior along the learning journey and is especially important during times of disappointment.

At lunch, the pastor tells me he has finished reading almost all of Dietrich Bonhoeffer's works. He hasn't read *Sanctorum Communio* yet, but he just turned the last page of the *Christmas Sermons.* Beginning in Lent, the council is going to read *Life Together*. The congregation recently made a commitment to articulate the values that would guide their decisions about mission giving. "We started working on the list, but then decided we shouldn't continue until we read *Life Together*," the pastor explained.

This pastor leads a congregation that is sturdy. It isn't likely to be the focus of a church growth study, or make the cover of *USA Today* during Holy Week. However, it is a congregation that makes a difference in people's lives. The parking lot is full during the week. The lights are on in the evening. Membership numbers are steady, while worship attendance is increasing.

Congregations are *religious* bodies, having to do with the things of God. Clergy and lay leaders face all kinds of challenges. In problem-solving mode, it is easy to forget the primary subject of a congregation. Likewise, clergy and lay leaders also face disappointment ("even after forming the new team, giving was down last year"). However, clearly recalling and consistently acting on the reality that God is the subject of the congregation provides congregations the energy and thoughtfulness needed to address their most pressing challenges and opportunities.

Religious coherence provides immunity against fearful reasoning. Through religious coherence there is greater congruence between a congregation's stated values and what it does. Such congruence strengthens the will of a congregation as it faces the inevitable challenges of conflict, cultural demands, and the wear and tear of everyday life.

People do not need to become theological experts in an academic sense. It is possible to overtheologize the design of the church office. Congregations do not need to host certificate programs in Barth's *Dogmatics*. Yet, congregations that practice what they preach, and preach what they practice, align thinking and action in a coherent manner, rooted in religious values. Such intelligibility strengthens a congregation against forces that otherwise might weaken ministry.

Congregational religious coherence constructs thinking about God that matches the reality of God and the congregation's experience of God. Some things are mystery, but not all things. Clergy and lay leaders make essential aspects of faith knowable by being articulate about God, and then shaping congregational life in ways consistent with what is being articulated.

In a religiously coherent congregation, thinking about God is rooted in a tradition. Yet, the tradition is corrected, supported, and otherwise influenced by the present context. What does this mean to us now?

Religious coherence takes many forms in a congregation. It might begin with a clergyperson's interest in a particular theological school of thought ("I've always been interested in Paul Tillich," or "I was changed by a visit to a Dorothy Day site in New York"). Or a congregation might have experience connecting with a particular theological movement ("believe it or not, we still have deep Scottish roots here; Knox would love us"). Theological coherence might get planted in a congregation because someone brings a book to a study group and its contents takes root with the readers ("we got started on this because we all read *Mere Christianity* together").

Such beginnings lead to strategic efforts to integrate theological reflection into the life of the congregation. This takes place formally at the governing board. Evidence of theological coherence might show up in mission and vision statements. It is supported by adult education. Religious coherence is exhibited informally as part of everyday conversation—prayer during hospital visits, comments in the hallway, Facebook messages, and so on.

Congregations that live by coherent theological themes might participate in pilgrimages (even if they don't call them that). They might collect relics (this cross was worn by our missionary in the Sudan). All such things contribute, not just to a theological opinion, but also to a comprehensive worldview.

After lunch, my pastor friend and I walked out into the sunlight. I asked, "What's going on back at the church?" He said, "Tonight I'm sitting in on a meeting about repaving the parking lot." I said, "I bet that doesn't have much to do with Bonhoeffer." He was turning toward his car when he said, "You'd be surprised. I always am."

RELIGIOUS WORLDVIEWS AND THEOLOGICAL CONVICTIONS

The religious coherence of a congregation is the culmination of study. It is also the culmination of testimony, behaviors, and practices that communicate a clear representation of your congregation's most valued religious claims and commitments. This does not mean that your congregation, that your congregants, all agree about religious values. Within any given congregation a variety of theological worldviews exist.[4] Some individuals in your congregation are incarnational; they are moved by the experience of the nearness of God. Others connect with transcendent experiences, feeling a part of something far beyond themselves. Some in your congregation find great value in the doctrinal statements of your religious tradition. It means everything to them to be reminded that God is sovereign. They miss it if the Apostles' Creed isn't recited during worship. Others find doctrinal statements lifeless; such folk might instead find meaning in good deeds. More differences: some of your congregants are agnostic, some, atheist; some have unconventional views of God. Even more differences: some of us move through these different theological worldviews during different seasons of our lives. There is significant diversity of theological thought in most congregations. This diversity is held deeply inside individuals but is not always expressed.

With all this variety, your congregation does have a culture of religious experience that is at least relatively coherent to most participants. It is not only educational but functional (as well as spiritual) to make more explicit the religious coherence that does exist. Why? It provides boundaries for normative behavior. No matter how inclusive we claim to be, it is a human reality that we, all of us, have limits to the differences we can manage in community.

Also, coherence provides positive energy when faced with disappointment. When dealing with disappointment, the congregation that has a sturdy theological framework upon which to rely is going to be more resilient. When a congregation is stymied in its attempt to learn something new, progress can occur when deeply held values align with learning. Perhaps the most powerful response to disappointment is to reconfirm your highest aspirations, to reaffirm what is at stake in the success of the endeavor.

Remember the congregation seeking to befriend the immigrant population. In the midst of reflecting on the challenges that practicing hospitality presented, Rev. Bartley recalls a moment of testimony:

> We had a refugee share her story about how she survived in the refugee camps. Tragically, her husband was murdered in front of her. She was thrown in jail. She didn't have a stitch of clothing, eight months pregnant. She gave birth in her cell by herself. She literally tied the umbilical cord off with hair from her head. She named the twins after the warden of the prison where she was. Two days later, the warden's wife showed up at her cell with clothing for the two children and for her and said, "When I heard that you honored my husband by naming your children after him, I wanted to meet you." Then she told how this woman went to her tea club and shared her story and it spread enough that a missionary heard it and said, "We need to do something." The missionary intervened and got her released. She told the story to our congregation and everybody was overwhelmed. I was able to ask the question, "Do you think maybe there's something about love and forgiveness that we can learn from this person?"

This very human story is a theological marker for the pastor and the congregation. It represents that endeavors like building sharing, kitchen sharing, and clean restrooms are almost always connected to a larger human narrative. The larger human narrative is connected to a religiously coherent framework that the congregation can claim despite disappointments. Love and forgiveness are theological values worth living despite setbacks. It also reminded the pastor why this was important to him. As religious leaders, we can travel through paths of disappointment more steadily if we remember what core values are aligned with our learning journeys.

The experience of disappointment is a passage along the learning journey inviting deeper theological reflection. Why does this matter to us? What human story is part of all that we are trying to do? What message is God providing us?

TOOLS

It is rarely instantaneously clear what religious concerns most coherently align with a congregational challenge, let alone a disappointment. This is acutely so if the congregational challenge is mundane. After all, how do you make the connection between faith in God and the need to repave the parking lot in order to repair cracks and potholes?

There are tools that you can apply during your learning journey to help you identify the religious claims and commitments at stake. Let's look at some of these tools.

W. Paul Jones has written a book titled *Worlds Within a Congregation.* This book provides a framework for thinking about the religious worldviews that exist in the congregation you serve. This is not an easy task. In most congregations, as noted above, there are a variety of religious understandings held by adherents. It is not necessary for everyone to agree. However, congregational learning is strengthened when diversity of thought is collated into something like a unifying point of view. The book by Jones names five theological views in a congregation. Each world represents an essential rhythm, which are

- separation and reunion,
- conflict and vindication,
- emptiness and fulfillment
- condemnation and forgiveness, and
- suffering and endurance [5]

By providing examples of these rhythms, Jones helps you think about ways to communicate a coalescing expression of faith in the midst of the diversity that exits. Additionally, the rhythms can assist you in more precisely naming any disappointment you are experiencing. Is the disappointment rooted in conflict? Then perhaps you can trace a narrative of vindication (or reconciliation). Is the disappointment creating a sense of emptiness? Then address the disappointment with fulfilling activities.

Another resource related to religious worldview and congregations is the book *Claiming Theology in the Pulpit* by Burton Cooper and John McClure.[6] Though the book specifically addresses concern about theological expression in the sermon, the inventory provided in the book can help you solidify language about a variety of theological claims concerning a variety of settings.[7] The inventory clarifies complex theological concepts. It invites you to think thoroughly about the language you use to express faith related to several theological categories: authority, theodicy, atonement, theism, endings, and others. After all, theological claims are made by congregations all the time, not just from the pulpit. Words, visuals, how food is served at congregational dinners, the way decisions are made, how visitors are greeted, and much more all express theological convictions.

VALUES

Clarity about values is another way that a congregation can promote a coherent religious worldview. Certainly, careful thinking about beliefs, doctrines, systems of theology, and Biblical interpretation are important and even essential. However, lived theology is often most evident in values that are expressed through behavior. Values that can be linked to congregational practice demonstrates not just theological claims, but also actual commitments. Note the values in the table below. Circle no more than four that are enacted by your congregation. Consider: How do these values connect with what your congregation is seeking to address?

The value exercise can be done with the team most responsible for the challenge. Ask team members to identify the top four values that relate to the project. See which values show up more than once. Consider these questions:

What congregational stories relate to these values?
What stories relate to the challenge?
What scripture narratives relate to these values and challenge?
How do you manage disappointment regarding these values?
How have these values been affirmed and promoted in the congregation?
What is at stake if one of the top values is demoted?
In what ways do the named values represent competing commitments?
How can the discussion about values be shared with more people in the congregation?

Values

Abundance	Empathy	Love	Teamwork
Adventure	Family	Mystery	Transcendence
Appreciation	Friendliness	Nonconformity	Trust
Awe	Fun	Obedience	Uniqueness
Belonging	Generosity	Order	Warmth
Calmness	Grace	Piety	Wonder
Candor	Gratitude	Pragmatism	Care
Growth	Reflection	Compassion	Holiness
Responsibility	Courage	Hospitality	Reverence
Curiosity	Humility	Self-Control	Imagination
Service	Diversity	Integrity	Simplicity

A COMPASS TO LEAD YOU AWAY FROM DISAPPOINTMENT

I am directionally challenged. I get lost driving to the grocery. Am I headed north or south? I'm grateful that our youngest son has an excellent internal compass. When we were visiting Washington, DC, he made sure we were able to get back to the National Mall from the Holocaust Museum. Otherwise I might still be sitting on the steps of the Lincoln Memorial waiting for direction.

In learning, as on a hike in an unmarked woods, it is helpful to have a compass. While hiking, the compass serves as a navigational instrument. With your congregation, the compass is a metaphor for that which keeps you moving in the right direction. A compass might be a resource that provides you with a reference point. A compass might be a book, a person, a saying, a passage of scripture that orients you and your colleagues to that which is most important about the congregational challenge.

In the context of a learning journey, the compass is a tool that contains the spiritual essence of the work taking place. A compass is another way of thinking about an outside resource. The compass is an image for using an outside resource combined with your congregation's ingenuity to keep the community on the best path regarding its challenge. Sometimes the compass is a mantra (remember how a mantra can be useful when defining your challenge). Sometimes the compass is an orienting Bible verse; sometimes it is a powerful theological claim. A compass can be a coach that knows just the right word to share with you in the right way at the right time. A congregation working on learning new hymns for worship used the saying attributed to St. Augustine, "A person who sings prays twice," as their compass. A congregation seeking to strengthen its culture of generosity used this story from one of its members as the compass:

> I was walking down the city street. A homeless person was sitting with a sign that simply said, "Please." I gave the person five dollars and said, "Be gentle with yourself." The person looked up at me and said, "Come closer." I leaned in closer." He whispered. I couldn't hear him. I said, "What?" He said, "God bless you." I said "Thank you." He touched my hand. He said, "No, really, I want you to understand God blesses you." He put a piece of paper in my hand. I moved on quickly feeling uncomfortable. A block down the road I opened my hand. I saw what he gave me. He gave me a ten-dollar bill.

For the congregation, this story functions like a compass directing people to generosity.

A congregation experimenting with starting an afterschool program for the children attending the public school across the street turned to Matthew 19:13–15 as their compass. Little children are brought to Jesus. The disciples wince. Jesus affirms the children. When a leadership team said that they sought to begin an afterschool ministry in order to offer God's love to the neighborhood children, one member objected by saying that the neighborhood children would not respect the church building. The pastor offered an interpretation of Matthew 19 observing that the children depicted in this encounter were likely street children, maybe orphans, who were welcomed unconditionally by Jesus. The pastor noted that the children had much to offer the congregation in terms of hope. The scripture passage, now referred to often, kept the conversation about the potential program rooted in aspirational values and not fear. A compass, in this case an orienting text, can keep you going in the right direction.

What compass is orienting your congregation about a particular challenge right now? This compass can guide you when things get difficult.

I WONDER . . .

Another way to encourage clarity about faith and the challenge you are addressing is to ask leaders to respond to "I wonder " questions (they look like statements but function as questions) related to the challenge. "I wonder" questions are expressions of the art of conversation, one of the key behaviors for navigating a learning journey. They are helpful responses to disappointment (or just plain unknowing) because they open up the imagination. In the face of disappointment, it is helpful to think in terms of possibilities through resourceful conversation.

I was introduced to "I wonder" questions through the book *Young Children and Worship* by Sonja Stewart and Jerome Berryman.[8] In their book, story experiences with scripture are followed by a variety of "I wonder" questions about each Bible story. Such questions encourage conversation. They are open-ended, so they are not prescriptive. They improve the prospect of locating the experience of God within the experience of learning taking place in the congregation.

Here are some examples:

I wonder how God is at work in this endeavor.

I wonder what scripture informs our approach to this challenge.

I wonder what scripture might challenge our approach to this challenge.

I wonder what gifts God is giving us to accomplish this.

I wonder what means of grace are available to us.

I wonder what our prayer is about this learning journey so far.

I wonder what glimpses of God we've seen along the way.

I wonder what God may be giving us permission to let go of.

I wonder how God is active in a recent disappointment related to our learning.

I wonder what statement in a recent sermon speaks to our situation.

I wonder what recent inspiration might be God's still, small voice.

I wonder what this disappointment reminds us of.

I wonder how we are making sense of the good and bad.

I wonder what value is most at stake right now.

I wonder what one thing we can do next.

I wonder what outside helper would provide us the most learning at this time.

"I wonder" questions like these can help you and your colleagues consider what matters most to you, even when you are experiencing disappointment.

Religious coherence, expressing a spiritual essence related to your challenge, can lead you out of disappointment to consider next steps. Your next steps might be, "No. We aren't going to take this further." Or your response might be a "not yet," or a resilient "yes." Let's consider these possible responses.

RESPONSES TO DISAPPOINTMENT

The old detective novel *Trent's Last Case* by E. C. Bentley begins with the sentence, "Between what matters and what seems to matter, how should the world we know judge wisely?"[9] Disappointment necessitates wise judgments. How will you proceed when things haven't gone as hoped? After all, this isn't just a project you are working on, it is a learning journey.

A "no" means that you will not pursue the learning. You will stop the process. You will move on to other endeavors. There are many conditions that would lead to a "no." These conditions include a loss of interest. It is difficult for congregations to remain focused even on the things that are going well. If disappointment is paired with lack of interest, this should lead to a "no."

Sometimes congregations stop a learning process because something more important needs attention. A congregation was set to begin a new building program. An architect had drawn up conceptual drawings. Then a flood hit their urban area. It directly affected their building. The flood waters rendered many surrounding buildings unusable. This particular congregation took on several community services: a weekly meal, twelve-step groups, and so forth. The governing board learned that they valued their neighbors needs more than the plans for the new building. They said "no" to the new construction and concentrated on expanding community engagement.

Other disappointing circumstances can result in a "no." Pastoral transitions can lead a congregation to stop developing a new idea; so can economic downturns. A board might decide that a proposed project doesn't align with the values of the congregation. This can be discouraging to some congregants. One congregation stopped a project related to a pastor's sabbatical when a grant wasn't approved.

If your congregation, as a result of a disappointment, is going to stop a learning journey, be clear about that decision. Share it with all involved. Frame it rationally. Don't overexplain, yet share the practical wisdom shaping the decision. Articulate why this makes sense theologically for your congregation, too. Name the values that shaped the decision. Share the commitments that are being kept regarding other initiatives.

Sometimes a disappointment leads to a "not now" response. A congregation had started on expanding a project in which several members were being trained to offer special care to congregants facing the end of life. Expanding this special care involved offering services to those in the community who did not have a congregational home. When the leader of the project, sadly, experienced a grave illness, the congregation put a hold on their plans. However, in honor of the project leader, they promised one another that they would pick up the plans within the year. "Not now" is a response that respects the reality that things happen that we had not planned. We are not always in control of scheduling our learning. It is important that a "not now" response be authentic. Such a response should not be a way to avoid saying "no" or avoiding essential work. It should be in response to discerning the right time to accomplish the right thing in the right way.

A congregation can respond to disappointment by getting back on track. This is a "yes" response. This is resilience. The journey may be different than originally planned. After all, disappointment sharpens focus.

Remember the congregation that built the playground but then had no children running to the slide and swings. During a time of theological reflection, one of the longtime members asked a group, "What about babies? Where are the babies?" From that question came a renewed interest in reaching out to families with children. The congregation dedicated itself to beginning a daycare. This started a new learning journey in which the congregation more precisely defined their challenge, sought help from outside resources, and started a daycare that was fully subscribed in the first year. Every weekday, there are now children running in the playground. Now there are children present in worship when previously there had been none.

The honoring of disappointment is a recognition of the ambiguity that exists in congregational efforts, even more so in the ones that matter the most. Even the best of ideas in a congregation will have intended and unintended negative consequences. Yes, Eden was the home of the tree of the knowledge of good and evil. There was a time in my life when I didn't believe that a place as fine as Eden could hold both good and evil. Don't tell me there is anything bad in Eden. I don't want to hear it.

Yet in the middle of all our congregational endeavors there is good and evil, or at least good and bad. There is the bitter with the sweet, the good times and the bad times, the rough and the smooth, sickness and health. There is plenty and want, rise and fall, death and resurrection. A significant task in life is making sense of having both good and bad together in the same room at the same time. Part of coming to terms with life is holding both the positive and negative simultaneously.

This is also true in trying to accomplish new things in your congregation. God helps us make sense of good and bad not by shielding us from the bad, but by giving us God's self as a way to metabolize the good and bad together.[10] That is, by faith we learn that we can experience fully both the good and bad in life knowing that we can hold on to the good while making sense of the bad. Don't let yourself fall into thinking that your congregational endeavors are all or nothing propositions. Challenge yourself when you start thinking that way. Know that it is theologically coherent to find life and love and grace and hope and the best outcome in any given endeavor, no matter the situation.

You know you are experiencing the disappointment of a learning journey when the following occur:

- Something unexpected happens that leads you to rethink the validity of the project.
- You realize the challenge you face is much larger than your congregation's capacity.
- A mistake has been made that hinders progress to the extent that you wonder if it's worth it.
- You recognize that the results you were hoping for aren't occurring.

- A person key to the success of the endeavor is no longer available.

Questions to ask when you are aware of disappointment include the following:

- What are we learning from this?
- What conditions and factors contributed to this frustration?
- Is this disappointment communicating "no," "not yet," or "yes"?
- What was the goal in the first place? Does that still hold true?
- What are our key religious claims and commitments related to this? Has this changed?

Things you can do when in the midst of disappointment include the following:

- Be clear with yourself and others about the disappointment.
- Think theologically about what matters most to you and your congregation.
- Consider the primary values your congregation holds.
- Use a conceptual framework for reflection like the ones from Cooper and McClure or Jones noted in this chapter.
- Ask "I wonder" questions about the future.
- Reframe disappointment as natural, not as all or nothing.
- Work toward a decision regarding "no," "not yet," or "yes."

Chapter Six

Discovery

Discerning the Best Solution

Have you had a *this is it* experience as part of your congregation? You were working on an important project. You knew the key question. You defined the challenge. You talked with people who traveled down a similar path. Still, you weren't sure what to do to make the project a reality. Maybe the idea didn't quite fit your congregation's story. Or, maybe you couldn't see how the new idea could take hold without giving up something very dear to your faith community.

Then it happened. You were in a meeting. Somebody said something that had the affect of clearing the path of a large tree that had been blocking your way ahead. "This is it," you thought. You now knew where you were going to lead the congregation. This is the right thing. No more sleep loss. No more disappointment. Time to move ahead with a strong-hearted "yes." The path was straight beyond the bend.

In story after story about congregations that have accomplished what they set out to do, there is a "this is it" experience. This experience might be called an "aha moment." Some call it a "eureka" flash. In terms of the learning journey, there is a *discovery*. There is an experience in which congregational leaders see, find, or become aware of the way forward as if for the first time.

You may have heard of this old story. It involves the ancient Greek genius Archimedes.[1] He lived long ago, more than two hundred years before the birth of Jesus of Nazareth. Yes, he was a genius. He did more than dabble in many subjects. He deeply explored mathematics, astronomy, engineering, and much more. The king presented him with a challenge. The king had a new crown made out of gold provided by the king himself. Yet, there was something about this crown that bothered the king. It didn't seem quite right. Was it that it appeared not as shiny as he expected? Or maybe it was supposed to be thicker around the back edges? The king suspected the goldsmith had substituted some lesser material for the gold the king had provided. "Figure this out," he said to Archimedes.

Though Archimedes was a genius, he didn't know how to help the king. He held gold in one hand and the crown in the other. What to do? The weight of the crown seemed to be the same weight as the amount of gold the king had provided. But he could hear the doubt of the king, "Something's not right."

Archimedes worked on many projects at a time. He decided to move on for the time being. He had other things that required his attention. One day he decided to take a bath (back then in a public setting, of course). Unfettered by other cares, he approached the water tub. As he got in the tub the water overflowed. "This is it," he thought. Or in proper Greek, "Eureka," he shouted as he jumped out of the tub (no time for a robe) and ran through the streets calling his glee for all to hear.

He had figured out the challenge. In a moment of insight his brain became aware of the difference between weight and volume. The weight of an object is how heavy it is. The volume of an object is the amount of space it takes up. Different materials of the same weight have different volumes (think feathers versus gold). Objects put in water will displace water. The displaced water is equal to their volume.

Archimedes set up an experiment with two bowls in which he measured the volume of the water displaced. He measured the volume of water displaced by the crown. Then he measured the volume of water displaced by a gold block of the same weight. The crown displaced more water. Aha, the goldsmith had substituted different metals. Busted! All of this discovered by a flash of insight, a moment of discovery.

Sometimes the discovery moment is obvious. The church council had been talking for what seemed like years about how often to have communion. They provided the Lord's Supper during worship ten times a year. Some on the council thought this practice should stay the same. Some thought it should change. This included people who thought communion should be part of worship more times a year, some fewer. The pastor had the council study communion practices. They read a book by William Willimon titled *Sunday Dinner*.[2] The pastor said, "It has some years on it but so does the Lord's Supper!" The council administered a congregational survey. They invited a seminary professor to come speak at an evening study gathering. The study helped.

Yet, the moment of discovery was revealed in a personal encounter. It was in that moment the pastor knew it was right to offer communion every week. He knew this when the oldest worshiper came up to him after communion was served one Sunday and said, "This is why I get these old eighty-five-year-old bones out of bed to go to church." The pastor said that if communion was what (let's call her) Miss Eleanor needed every week, who was he to keep it from her? The pastor shared this story with the council. The leaders voted after ten minutes of discussion (and the previous year of study) to host communion every Sunday. Miss Eleanor had provided them with their moment of discovery.

Discoveries happen in the space between people. A woman was telling me about how the congregation she attends began a counseling center. She recalls the several months she spent picking up and driving a young woman to worship. The young woman had been diagnosed with schizophrenia. She had stopped into the church office for help with her utility bill. After she received a voucher she was invited to worship and said, "Yes!" Transportation was arranged. On their drives to and from church, this lay leader learned about the woman's good and bad days, the medicines she was on, the counseling she received (or more accurately, the counseling she wasn't receiving). One day when our storyteller asked her new friend if she had found a new counselor, her friend said, "Yes, it's you." "Right at that moment," said the lay leader, "little did I know that I would be spending the next three years forming a team and developing a licensed counseling center out of our building."

This is it moments—moments of discovery—are the pivot points where an idea moves from exploration to action steps and implementation.

CONGRUENT AND DISRUPTIVE DISCOVERIES

Scripture is abundant with revelation. Scripture is abundant with experiences that reveal the presence or intentions of God. We know that moments of revelation recorded in scripture represent occasions when something transcendent occurred. Your view of scripture may include the understanding that events in scripture happened just as they are related to us. Or, your view of scripture may be that moments of revelation signify a truth that goes beyond what actually occurred or didn't occur, yet still reveals a blessed reality about life. Behind and beyond the transcendence (and sometimes incredibility) of scriptural aha moments is the actuality that people of faith have experienced moments of clarity on their path of learning.[3]

Some discoveries are congruent with the long journey that has come before. Such discoveries represent the accumulation of sacred leadings. Cleopas and his friend are taking the seven-mile hike from Jerusalem to Emmaus (Luke 24:13–32). They experience Jesus as a stranger. Their experience with this stranger includes a recital of the Jesus story. At the first-mile marker there is conversation of Jesus's death. By the third-mile marker the conversation turns to the empty tomb. These conversations represent an exploration of Jesus's life. By the fifth mile, Jesus, still known only as a stranger, takes more initiative in the dialogue. He recalls the stories of Moses, the prophets, indeed of Israel. At the seven-mile mark they find a diner. Bread is blessed. It is broken. It is shared (Miss Eleanor would be pleased). Cleopas and friend recognize Jesus. This is *him*. This is it.

Some moments of discovery are consistent with what has already occurred on your journey—with the experiences you've had. When the pastor heard Miss Eleanor's affirmation of the Lord's Supper, that was a revelation consistent with the congregation's exploration. It was not dissimilar. After all, they had been studying the subject. Congregational leaders were well into a discernment process related to the frequency of celebrating the Lord's Supper. It wasn't like something entirely new had been revealed to them. If anything, Miss Eleanor's comment made visible something that had already been present in their community—the positive connection that communion represented for congregants. It was as if the council was already headed in the direction of affirming the importance of the sacrament. They just didn't know it yet. In retrospect, everything became clearer. Such is the way many eureka moments will function in your congregation. Such moments will affirm a reality that makes perfect sense, once the revelatory experience has occurred. Before, the clarity or creativity or courage may be lacking. After, things will be as they are supposed to be, moving forward to accomplish something new and good.

The spark of recognition for Cleopas and friend at the breaking of the bread made perfect sense at that moment. At that moment their experience of Jesus at the table in Emmaus was entirely consistent with their experience of Jesus in Jerusalem. The moment of revelation was supported by experiential harmony. This Jesus was the same as that Jesus. Congruency reinforced the revelation.

However, some discovery experiences can be disruptive. Think of another road, not the road to Emmaus. This is the road to Damascus (Acts 9). Saul is walking this road. Saul was known for his terrorist-like attitude toward those who followed Jesus. Saul would have hunted Cleopas, not had lunch with him. But as you know (when did you first hear this story?) along the way to Damascus a light from the sky shone around him as he fell to the ground. Indeed, God grounded Saul. God made Saul blind to his old life and ready for a new life. God grounded Saul by giving him a new foundation on which to stand. This was revelation. This was discovery. This was an aha moment.

It was disruptive. This was disturbing, too. Saul became the primary, public supporter of the Jesus movement. His support had the same intensity as his previous opposition. People who knew Saul (or was it Paul?) must have asked, "Is this the same guy?"

Sometimes your congregational revelations are going to be unsettling. They will spin you and send you in a different direction. Things will happen you hadn't expected. You might ask, "Is this the same church?"

For years, a pastor in a Midwest small town had said, "Not on my watch," every time the possibility of selling their old, historic building came up in conversation. One council member said (rather frequently), "We are spending all our time fixing the building, none of our time building disciples." Then one Sunday morning worshipers turned the lights on in the darkened sanctuary to find much of the tall ceiling had fallen on the pews. The pastor thought to himself, "I guess it is going to be on my watch." Years later he said, "I don't think my theology would say that God caused that ceiling to fall, but I do think it was a revelation for me."

Not all moments of discovery are comforting. George Hunsinger, commenting on the theology of Karl Barth, writes, "Grace that is not disruptive is not grace. . . . Grace, strictly speaking, does not mean continuity but radical discontinuity."[4] For some congregations, maybe yours, an aha moment is going to be like a conversion experience. The current inspiration will lead to a future that is discontinuous with the past. Be careful. This is holy ground. It might be holy ground set afire by something like a lightning strike.

In certain situations, almost any moment of discovery is going to be incongruent with the past. A congregation was dying. To say the congregation was dying was to acknowledge that its members were dying. There were no young newcomers to replace them. This congregation had existed since 1865. It was not realistic to think the congregation would be functioning five years in the future. This is not an easy thing to acknowledge. It is upsetting to be the one who knows there isn't going to be a future for your worshiping community. It is upsetting to be the pastor who has to close the doors. It is one thing to read a statistic. It is another to be the statistic. The social science research does not capture this kind of pain. "My congregation is going to close. I feel so sad."

There is anticipatory grief related to the death. Members, clergy, judicatory representatives, and others connected to the congregation experienced the grief. Pain has also occurred because of the natural desire to delay the loss that goes with closing a congregation. That is, the closing of the congregation has been hindered partially to fend off the understandable pain of actual loss. Extended hospice stays can be excruciating. Perhaps this is predictable. There may be no other way than the long way. We are not good at embracing loss. How could we be?

None of this was going through the mind of the pastor one evening when he was working on his sermon at the church. It also happened to be the night when Alcoholics Anonymous met weekly in the fellowship hall. He was always conscientious to say "hello" to those present (when he was there), but not hang around. He knew confidentiality was important to this group in this small town. But on this night a gentleman wanted to talk to him. "Hey, pastor, do you know of any place in town for a halfway house for our guys who are just starting recovery?"

The pastor said, "No," but he would keep it in mind. Which he did. For the next several weeks he couldn't get the question off his mind: "Do you know of any place in town?" He took the question to his small council of leaders. The initial response was, "No, we don't know of any place."

The pastor then looked for the gentleman who had asked him the question (staying late at the church two weeks in a row even when he had no need to). Each time the gentleman was nowhere to be found. The pastor thought to himself, "Maybe he was just an angel."

At the next council meeting one of the leaders on the council, just before adjournment, said, "Remember last meeting about there being a place for a halfway house? I don't know if this is the right thing or not, but maybe it is time for us to start thinking about what this building is going to be in five years, because I don't think it is going to be a church."

There was silence. One person began to cry.

In the blink of an eye, some revelations begin the journey of disruptive change—possibilities that differ greatly from the past. Perhaps your discovery moment is not just disruptive, it might also be disturbing. Then again maybe it also holds your attention and will not go away.

In this way your discovery might function like some Biblical parables. As we now know, parables aren't just simple tales that reinforce the status quo. Jesus's parables were often received as disruptive revelation, particular to those first listeners. Think of it, a mustard shrub compared to the Kingdom of Heaven. Whatever happened to the great cedars of Lebanon? Or a parable about a hidden treasure in a field that was bought by the happy finder. It was like winning the lottery! Except for one small detail. John Dominic Crossan argues that first-century real estate law would have had that glorious treasure returning to the original owner.[5] Or the Good Samaritan (really the Bad Samaritan to the original audience) saving the person in the ditch—who, based on audience response criticism, could have been no one other than, yes, the original listener. Thus, a disruptive revelation—the very one you despise—holds your life in his or her hands.

If you are trying to accomplish something new in your congregation, you will likely have a moment of discovery. And on occasion your moment of discovery may signal more than just something new. It may signal something *radically* different for your faith community.

ALL ALONG THE JOURNEY

Another way to think about moments of discovery is that they occur all along the learning journey. An aha experience isn't just a one-time occurrence. While you are trying to define your challenge, your group might have a eureka moment during which, for the first time, the articulation of the challenge is clear. "Oh, this project isn't about our building, it is about getting clear about who we are as a people of God."

While you are exploring the challenge you might come across the exact right resource, seemingly by accident. Let's say your congregation is working on a strategic planning process, but you aren't sure exactly what the process should be. You go online looking at books on planning. You read an article on how you should start. You think to yourself, "This isn't it." A pastor friend gives you a book on planning for congregations. As you describe it to a board member she says, "This all sounds so negative." Then, one day you are talking to a neighbor who in an offhand way describes an exercise she participated in at her workplace (the local public health department). She calls it "asset mapping."[6] She is smiling the whole time she describes what fun the process was. Later that day you go to Amazon and read about asset mapping (there are several books). You think, "This is it." Sometimes while you are exploring the landscape of your challenge you will have a moment of discovery.

Sometimes the moment of discovery arrives while you are taking on the new endeavor. Sometimes the aha moment arrives just in time for implementation. Recall the congregation exploring new possibilities around Sunday School. Rev. Teri Thomas had told her leaders that "Sunday School was dead." So they worked on defining their challenge. They explored the environment for opportunities. What could Christian education for children look like now? There were disappointments along the way. They had a plan related to the arts. The children would have the opportunity to respond to the sermon scripture of the day through art, music, drama, dance, creative writing—even mission. Despite the new plan, there was a significant problem. No one came. During the Sunday School hour, the place to be was the gathering place: a wonderful, new space in the building that contained the draw of coffee, donuts, and good conversation.

The team's first thought was, "We need to shut down coffee hour." After more conversation someone shared a spark of insight, "No, we move the program into the gathering place where the coffee, donuts, and people already are."

This discovery didn't solve all their challenges. It did provide the team the energy (and hope) to move ahead with implementation. The reality of a busy and a bit messy gathering space on Sunday was significantly more compelling than empty, 1960s-style classrooms.

CREATION ALIVE WITH REVELATION

God has created a world of plenty. It may seem that moments of revelation are scarce; that is what discovery is: revelation. However, sometimes it is that we haven't cultivated the expectation that revelations are part of the everyday structure of life. Sometimes aha moments from life beyond the congregation—family, work, play—can be transferred to congregational learning. Out of this transference comes learning that guides your faith community's inventive accomplishments.

Too often we differentiate too severely the dynamics of discovery for an individual from the dynamics of discovery for a community. This is an unhelpful separation.

A person goes on vacation to discern whether or not she is going to continue her work as a pediatrician. Should she retire now or work for a few more years? She still loves her work. But she is tired. She doesn't like managed care protocols. Then again, she feels needed each time she soothes a parent with a solution to a child's illness. So, she walks a trail in a state park. She is surrounded by the music of birds. She can hear the leaves like the sound of a soft brush on a Zildjian cymbal. The voice of her mentor comes back from memory, "If you love what you do but aren't doing what you love, change *how* you are doing it." Yes, a moment of discovery. This person now has insight regarding making vocational decisions. Perhaps one day she will transfer her insight to a conversation about congregational vocation.

The dynamics of revelation that we experience regarding other life realms are not different from the dynamics of revelation we experience in our worshiping communities. Aha moments come to individuals in similar ways that they come to communities; after all, communities are made up of individuals. Call them "eureka moments," or "this is it" occasions, or "moments of discovery"; such revelations are often revealed during times when one's guard is let down, away from the pressure of having to have an answer—away from the congregation itself.

At least this was Mark Knowles's experience. As a staff member of a Disciples of Christ congregation Mark was given the opportunity to reconstruct the way in which the congregation engaged the community. Before he was the director of outreach for the congregation, he served in the Peace Corps. And he was a grandson. Insights from both these roles helped him picture a resourceful way of thinking about outreach and service.

It doesn't matter if it has to do with international aid or serving your community through your congregation, sometimes our desire to do something big and glorious can get in the way. Though it is popular in some settings to think big, thinking big is sometimes a gateway to disappointment. What is it called? Right, the Big Hairy Audacious Goal is often something you plan during a structured process.[7] But just because an idea is big doesn't make it a revelation. It can be exciting. And it can keep you stuck. Mountains don't move overnight.

Years before Mark worked on community outreach for his congregation, he was standing in the middle of a small town in El Salvador. From where he stood, he saw a village of about four hundred people. Yet, the number zero was the controlling factor, as in no road, no electricity, no relationships. The community was deeply divided. The challenge in the form of an evocative question was, "How do you get things done in a community that is deeply divided, where there are various feuds going on all the time?"

The hope was that a large-scale project could change all the dynamics for the better. That was the plan. But Mark had an insight. Civil wars were fought over the very divisions represented in the community. There just wasn't the relational capacity to address an audacious goal. So the particular flash of insight was, "Let's change the goal—that is, as an outsider I can't fix the roads and the electricity, but I can help with the relationships."

This discovery involved an adjustment of scale. Mark started a project that involved nine groups of three families (not the entire community). The result of the project was to be the construction of stoves for homes. So, there wasn't going to be electricity for the entire village. But there would be safe stoves for twenty-seven households, a device to create supper and the connections that come with family meals. Another discovery was that though the visible output of the project was represented by stoves, the lasting impact was about relationships. Mark would help facilitate relationships by having the multiple families work together on this modest, common project.

Some revelations uncover the possible. Such revelation can be more powerful than audacious quests. The revelation of the possible leads to authentic accomplishment. Remember, Mark's role is defining community outreach anew with and for the congregation he serves. He is exploring the landscape of possibilities. Who do we partner with? What needs should be addressed? This isn't El Salvador. There are roads. There is electricity. There are stoves. But there are also lonely people with names. And a yearning for connection.

Some discoveries come while working in a foreign land. Some come from a conversation with someone who has known you your entire life. Mark is visiting his grandmother. He is not thinking about a congregation; he is thinking about his grandma. They are having lunch together. Midway through lunch she says, "Oh, I'm glad you are here. I want you to help me clean some stuff out in the garage." The two of them go to the garage. Mark moves boxes and he notices that there were some boxes perilously perched. He rearranges. He cleans. He talks with his grandma. After all, the objects contain stories. The ten-minute project becomes three hours.

Afterward, grandma says, "Well, I'm so glad you did that."

Mark responds, "I'm glad I could help." And then, "Grandma, surely there's somebody at your church that could help you out with this type of thing, right?"

She said, "Well, I don't feel comfortable asking about that."

Aha!

Now, Mark is thinking about the congregation he serves. This discovery moment holds an entire course of thoughts. He thinks again about small-scale connections. He thinks how this time with his grandma isn't just about moving boxes, but also about relationships. Mark reflects on how he probably received more from his visit with his grandmother than she did, though it was certainly helpful to move boxes so they didn't fall on her.

The thoughts keep moving toward him. Could our congregation do something like this for people? It isn't just about service. It is about attachments. The same value that was ultimately expressed through the construction of stoves in El Salvador: small groups of people working together to solve small problems and build sturdy relationships.

In Mark's case, moments of revelation in two very different contexts had the compounding effect of reinforcing a key value related to service. It is about relationships. Moments of discovery often develop from experiences beyond the congregations we serve. We serve our faith community well when we make connections between discoveries that occur beyond our congregations and the life of our faith community.

A COHERENT THEOLOGY OF REVELATION

At this particular moment Lillian (we will call her) is wishing she hadn't mentioned God. She sits in the pastor's office. With her is the pastor along with a member of the congregation named (let's go with) Klaus. Klaus is upset. He is upset because during Sunday worship, Lillian represented the capital campaign team by offering an announcement about raising 2.5 million dollars for repairs and enhancements of their historic building. The stained glass needs reinforcement. There is no elevator. The roof is thirty years old. The parking lot has more divots than the face of the moon. During her announcement Lillian said, "God wants you to give generously." It wasn't in her text. She just said it.

Now, Klaus is addressing Lillian and their pastor. "How do you know God wants us to give generously? Do you have a special line to God?"

Moving ahead on an important congregation project almost always involves a moment of insight. Because congregations are religious communities it is natural to connect such moments of insight to God. The theological category for this is revelation. Like most theological realities, revelation is contested territory. One person's revelation is another person's camouflage. Such a gap is difficult to resolve.

One way to address such a gap is to help your congregation hold a coherent theology of revelation. This relates to one of the primary behaviors of a learning congregation: articulating religious coherence. This doesn't mean that everyone in the congregation will have the same understanding of discovery and revelation. It does mean that in a learning congregation leaders will be articulate about revelation. Conversation about discoveries and decisions should be lucid. Obscurity is not helpful. Discussion of discoveries should be evocative. They should evoke a response, preferably a positive emotional response. You can't manipulate this as a leader. You can be humble, winsome, and eloquent in describing to others the discoveries experienced. You can observe the ways in which people vary regarding their experiences of revelation. People experience God's disclosures in different ways. Providing descriptions for these differences helps people be more considerate of the epiphanies of others.

Moments of discovery exist in different provinces. One way to think of discovery is in terms of four dimensions. Picture a chart, a four-quadrant matrix. At the top of the chart are two contrasting dimensions: immanence and transcedence. These represent God's proximity. Immanence represents an epiphany that is important yet characteristic of every day life. It will include the experience of God as among us, even one of us, not as wholly other. It will include the closeness of God. Transcendence represents a moment of discovery characterized by a sense of God's direction coming from above and beyond. The epiphany might well represent something existing beyond the limitations of the material universe. Something about the message goes beyond ordinary experience. God is wholly other than human.

At the left side of the chart are two other contrasting dimensions: special revelation and natural revelation. These represent God's means of revelation. Special revelation includes discoveries that come your way via scripture, the sacraments, or some other activity that is distinctly part of your religious tradition. Natural revelation includes aha moments that come your way through the world, through representations that are not overtly religious: a rainbow, the sound of the trees, a still small voice as you fall asleep.

Here are some examples.

Immanence/Special: The care committee is deciding whether or not to spend the year with a special emphasis on attention to those who have lost loved ones. The lay leader begins the meeting reading a thank you note from a grandmother who lost her grandson much, much too early. In the note the grandmother quotes Psalm 23 from memory, "Even though I walk in the shadow of death, you are with me." Her next sentence is, "I know God is with me because of the calls and visits

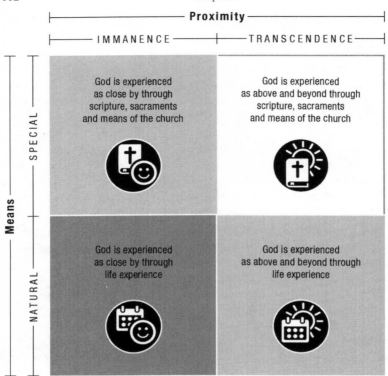

Figure 6.1.   Moments of Discovery. Moments of Discovery depicts four ways that an aha moment may be revealed during the learning journey. Being able to name the kind of revelation gives credence to the experience as you share it with others.

from my church friends." The silence after the letter speaks clearly, "Special attention to those who have lost love ones is the right thing to do."

Immanence/Natural: It is your choice. You are working on a team, but it is clear because of your role and function as clergy person that the team is looking to you regarding the decision as to whether or not to include a 15 percent mission goal in the upcoming capital campaign for the new sanctuary. You have gone to sleep deciding "yes." The next morning at Starbucks you are leaving with a grande coffee in your hand. You overhear a couple walking by you so closely they both brush against you. One says to the other, "Trust your feelings." Now, you *know* you have made the right decision.

Transcendence/Special: During worship you experience a sense of being swept away by God. You feel tears begin to flow. The hymn "When in Our Music God Is Glorified" leads you to know that the time is right to pursue the children's summer music camp.

Transcendence/Natural: While you are walking with a neighbor, the sun breaks through the clouds in a way that makes you feel you are in the midst of an uncharted, mystical kingdom. There is a rainbow in the distance. You've been talking with your friend about a vision for a new community ministry that involves partnering with an inner city congregation. Your friend points to the landscape and says, "It seems to me that God is leading you to the light."

You might desire to test your discovery. One way to test your discovery is to check it against another quadrant on the discovery matrix. If your aha moment has come to you through natural revelation, explore themes in scripture (special revelation) that might confirm and challenge your discovery. If your realization is strongly transcendent, check the message against the closeness of God.

Remember Klaus addressing Lillian and their pastor: "How do you know God wants us to give generously? Do you have a special text message line to God?" As the pastor knows, Klaus isn't much for scripture. And though he is active in the church he has an honest aversion to people speaking for God. The pastor discerns this. He decides not to quote scripture. He chooses not to appeal with that which is transcendent. Instead, he acknowledges Klaus's rebuttal. He empathizes. Lillian adds, "I can understand if you disagree with me, but I couldn't help it, I just spoke from my heart." Klaus leaves the conversation, no more convinced of the project, but satisfied that he was heard, and as a result chooses to keep his doubt to himself and trust the process. The interaction doesn't produce a miracle. It does produce learning. Lillian learns that it is risky to invoke God even when it feels natural. Klaus learns that his congregational leaders value him enough to listen to him. No miracle, but such learning keeps the process moving ahead.

DISCOVERY AND THE ART OF CONVERSATION

Most of the time when we talk and listen with one another we are not talking about or listening for revelations. So we don't have much practice at expressing or taking in moments of discovery. You and I have more experience talking about routine things that happen to us on any given day. You and I have more experience listening for that which most aligns with our experience. Moments of discovery coming from the voice of another is not something that we are trained to investigate. Moments of discovery often do not align with our experience. We humans have often been at a loss for words to describe the sky breaking open and holy disclosure descending. Jesus is baptized. The world shakes. Your heart races. And when you tell others about it, unbelievers just shake their head. So, we resort to talking about the flight of a bird.

As a congregational leader you will want to develop your ability to talk about revelation. Discovery talk is evocative. This is not primarily cognitive communication. You want memories and feelings to be stirred in others. The reason you want memories and feelings to come to mind for others is that you want to prompt a response. Of course you want the response to be positive. But a negative response is preferred to indifference or to someone's not hearing or understanding the communication. With a negative response, at least the disclosure has been heard. Positive or negative, you are seeking an authentic reaction from another person with whom you are sharing a discovery. An authentic response is more likely to occur when what you say connects with something from your listener's life experience. What you say should bring to heart something deep within your listener.

In the illustration above, Klaus was not connecting with Lillian's offhand declaration of God's desire of giving generously. It made sense for the time being to turn to empathy so that Klaus might remain openhearted to the possibility.

On the other hand, recall Mark's experience with his grandmother. Mark's visit to his grandmother naturally and authentically evoked an idea for how congregational care might look in his congregation. It will be natural for others to resonate with Mark's story. Most all of us have family members who could use extra attention. Who can't connect with a young man's affection for his grandmother? The revelation becomes even more evocative when his desire for his grandmother is translated into the natural and helpful care he desires for those in his congregation. It is a beautiful thing, really, translating a revelation from family life into a hope for congregational life.

When working with revelation and discovery regarding something new your congregation seeks to do, find ways to describe your revelation and discoveries in evocative ways. Personal stories are effective. Such stories are effective because you are expressing emotion the experience evoked in you. The more here and now the emotion, the more powerful it is. Relationship networks may work okay with six degrees of separation, but the emotional resonance of revelation calls for a closer connection of something more like two degrees of separation. Don't tell me the vision of a missionary an ocean away—someone I will never meet. I want to know what God is disclosing to *you.*

Conversation involves both talking and listening. We all can improve our ability to comprehend a discovery when it is being shared. I know there are times when someone is sharing an aha moment and I'm listening in the same way that I listen to programming announcements on the radio. I take in whatever fact I need. That's all I hear. This works well listening to programming announcements. It is not a good way to listen for revelation. Most people will test their insights with you to see if you are listening. The test will include partial disclosure. Even congregants who are close to you are not going to risk full disclosure of a discovery if they don't trust you will catch the importance of what is being said. One of the best responses when hearing someone begin to tell you about something important they've learned about congregational life is to say, "Tell me more."

Sometimes people will tell you of discoveries when you least expect it. Revelations don't come at the perfect time in the committee meeting. They are not guaranteed to be shared during a deep conversation about life in the pastor's study. They occur when the kids are being picked up from choir. The best and brightest idea might be hinted at when you talk for literally ten seconds while you are coming and going at Panera. Don't let the moment pass. Don't think, I will circle back later. Why wait? At least be curious enough to stop long enough to hear the nature of the epiphany waiting to be shared.

DISCOVERY AND TIMING

Here is a brief word about the behavior of timing (measured pace) so important to congregational learning. Most revelations about the one thing that will most help your congregation arrive when you are thinking or doing something else. In terms of the measured pace of congregational learning, many revelations will arrive later than desired. You can't force them. You shouldn't force them. Don't manufacture a discovery. These things are gifts.

The fact that revelation is a gift doesn't mean that your hard work didn't contribute. These "this is it" discoveries typically show up after defining your challenge, finding and using helpful resources, exploring, and experiencing disappointment. When Northminster Presbyterian Church members had the revelation to turn their gathering space into Sunday School space, it was after many conversations, reaching out to the community, and the disappointing experience that something new might not work. A discovery may feel like it fell from the broken sky with no warning. In retrospect, you can see how God was guiding you to this revelation. In retrospect it is as if such discoveries are written in the stars, already present, just waiting for you to look up on the right night when the light is just right. Don't force it. You can't see the stars at 12 noon in the Midwest. You have to wait for the sun to set. You have to have lived the day.

MOVING ON FROM DISCOVERY

There comes a time when discovery leads to action. Let's say that your congregation has wanted to help parents with the inescapable struggles of raising children. Let's say that you have defined your challenge as "providing support to parents so as to help them learn and practice new skills and feel less alone." A team has looked through various approaches. The same team has made it through the disappointment that the number of potential volunteers is limited. People are willing to attend workshops on parenting. They just aren't sure how they can lend a hand. A small child's behavior in worship (she just can't sit still and be quiet and can you hardly blame her?) has led to a kind of revelation. *Look, who is going to help this parent if it isn't us?* Now it is time to take on the new program. These things just don't happen. Let's look at how they do.

You know you are experiencing the discovery phase of a learning journey when the following occur:

- An idea that solves a problem pops into your mind when you are not thinking about the project.
- Someone shares an idea and you think, "This is it, this is what we need."
- Someone shares an idea that no one or hardly anyone catches the first time, but curiosity is raised.
- You find a story you share draws an evocative emotional response from another.
- You observe a solution in one life arena (family, work, neighborhood) that is a good fit for the challenge you are learning about in your congregation.
- You are willing to tolerate uncertainty for a while rather than rush to an answer.

Questions to ask when you are moving through the experience of discovery include the following:

- How can this insight be applied to our congregational challenge?
- Can we pause and talk more about what was just said right now?
- What scripture story does this insight sound like?
- How is this idea disruptive to the way we live as a faith community?
- In what ways does this insight give us more energy or less energy for this endeavor?
- What objection might there be to this epiphany?

Things you can do when in the midst of discovery include the following:

- Stop long enough to hear what is not being said.
- Listen for the type of revelation being shared (special, natural, immanent, transcendent) and test it against an alternative type.
- Look for ways in which the discovery is consistent with other positive congregational experiences.
- Share the insight with more people and be curious with them about their response.
- Be ready to move to action once the way ahead is clear.

Chapter Seven

Taking On and Letting Go

The Tasks of Implementation

You can make someone do something. But you can't make someone *want* to do something. This is true for organizations, too. Which makes it true for congregations also. You serve your religious community well when you think about how to help the congregation learn to take on a new endeavor. The congregation has had its moment of discovery, its aha moment. Now it is time to move to implementation, the task of taking on a new project. This *taking on* is the work of making the discovery an activity. It is the recital of the task that heretofore has been a dream, a discernment, an idea not fully realized.

When a congregation learns to do something new, moments of unease lead to experiences of discernment and discovery. These moments and experiences are like the rehearsal of a musical piece. At some point, the rehearsal gives way to the actual performance.

On a practical level, the actual performance involves taking on specific tasks. It involves a variety of operational activities. You need to determine roles and functions, budgets and so forth (more on this soon). You also need to summon the resolve to follow through on spirited moments of revelation. Activities don't magically materialize. They require the employment of talent, but they involve more than that, too. The realization of a great idea requires curiosity on the part of leaders. There is still much to be learned about an idea. The learning happens when one begins to experiment; the learning occurs when one begins to do what is required.

A congregation started a refugee ministry. They had been asked to do so by a social agency. The values of the program aligned with their values. Their aha moment was largely a "why not?"—which, given the need, was good enough. God speaks in versions of "why not?" It is a proven way for the Divine to be active in ambivalence. A family was arriving in a few days. No one in the congregation had experience with meeting refugees, let alone differentiating needs from wants from legalities. However, the assigned leader was willing to immerse himself in doing *something*. "We'll figure this out," he said.

Doing is learning. It was Aristotle who wrote in the *Nicomachean Ethics*, "The things we have to learn before we do them, we learn by doing them." [1] Congregations that effectively implement new projects do so because leaders view the project not only in terms of project management, but also as learning—even if they don't use that language.

The most important virtues of religious life are learned by experience. Effective practices of offering or receiving forgiveness are learned by trying to do them well. Sometimes it goes well. You muster the right words at the right moment with a catch in your throat no matter how many times you practice. ("I'm sorry no, really, I was wrong and this shouldn't happen again.") Such words are preceded by other attempts that weren't as authentic. ("I'm sorry if you heard something I didn't intend.") If the essential virtues of religious life—forgiveness and so many others like generosity, forbearance, patience, and humility—require trial and error, not just a plan on paper, then the work of the congregation involves learning by experience, too. Though implementation of ideas around buildings, budgets, staffing, and much more may sound mundane, they are in no less in need of virtue, particularly the virtue of learning by experience.

Of course, thinking of taking on new endeavors as a learning activity suggests that not all new endeavors will go as planned. The Tower of Babel wasn't conceived as a monument to hubris; it wasn't constructed as a locale of confusion. The idea was to unify humanity. The result did not match the intent. (Was it really because God sought to confuse the people or was God the scapegoat for human mistrust?) Sometimes plans do not sufficiently support experience. When this is the case, your congregation might need to be flexible in its execution. Cognitive scientist Gary Klein calls this *flexecution*.[2] He writes, "People often change their plans and goals on the basis of what they learn during execution. They're making discoveries along the way by diagnosing the reasons they're failing or having difficulty. They're trying to achieve goals while simultaneously redefining them."[3] Your learning may lead to positive adaptation.

It did for a certain congregation hosting a small group for caretakers of older adults. The need came from many adults in the congregation who found themselves as the primary caregivers for aging parents. When the program was conceived, a concern was that people wouldn't share enough of what was going on in their lives. The concern was that the conversation would be too safe. (For example, "Mom called me last night to say that she was looking forward to playing cards tomorrow.") What happened instead was that the group was overly willing to share intimate details of life. The convener of the group was concerned that participants would regret sharing what might be construed as confidential information. The leader responsible for older-adult ministry helped the convener to reconstruct the purpose of the support group. The group came to a useable, shared understanding of the difference between a support/prayer group and a therapy group. Flexible revisiting of the purpose led to stronger execution. By sharing fewer intimate details but receiving *more* support, participants reported greater confidence in addressing the daily challenges of older-adult care.

Possibilities, ideas, and opportunities are numerous in your congregation. The challenge is deciding which inspiration to implement. Once you are ready to act on the right idea, you will experience challenges regarding how to do the work. If your congregation is like many others, it is a larger task to make the dream a reality than to receive the dream.

ESSIE AND THE PARENTING GROUP

Essie was in worship on Sunday morning. The sermon was about the community of Christians depicted in the Acts of the Apostles. In the sermon, the preacher emphasized the phrase, "For they shared everything in common." Essie thought of her mother who shared everything she owned with her children. Essie's mother not only shared her belongings, the things she owned, but words of wisdom, ways to live life well.

Essie thought of things that the church shared in common with others. She made a mental list of the ways in which the church building was shared with the community. Several Alcoholics Anonymous groups met at the church building during the week. The church was a polling place. At one time, wasn't there a Grandmother's Club that met regularly?

For whatever reason, her mind landed on the title of what was then a recent book by Hillary Clinton. The book was titled *It Takes a Village: And Other Lessons Children Teach Us.*[4] As an educator, the development of children was important to her. She thought, "We don't share the responsibility of parenting like we could."

This was her aha moment.

Essie had been serving on a strategic planning endeavor with other church leaders and they were brainstorming possible new programs. At that moment in worship, she realized what new program she wanted her church to create. Essie wanted a parenting program for the community.

When leaders take on a new challenge, they also need to learn *how* to implement it effectively. Such effective implementation includes understanding exactly what is to be done, naming the desired outcome, assigning roles and functions, establishing a timeline, communicating with the rest of the congregation, forming a budget (including raising funds), and breaking down the ideas to specific tasks. In other words, taking a dream to reality requires a lot of work.

LEARNING TO DO

Once Essie received blessings from both the strategic planning group and the church board, she needed to learn how to move her idea to action. She needed to find out how to take on the development of the program. This meant more than doing. It meant *learning* how to do.

There are many reasons why great ideas in congregations don't lead to great activities. Not all moments of discovery result in projects that support the purpose of a congregation. The spark of revelation does not guarantee works of glory.

Why is this so? It may be lack of focus. Starting new endeavors require resiliency, staying power that may not always be present. After all, volunteers in a congregation have other responsibilities. Children need attention. Older adult parents require visits. Work is stressful. So, some ideas that develop out of a learning journey are not realized because busy (and often stressed) people aren't able to give matters the attention required. This is a critique, but not a criticism. Real life matters compete for attention and that competition is often between multiple goods. Focus is a self-limiting factor. Not every good is realized.

Sometimes your congregation might not be able to move ahead with an epiphany for lack of resources. The lack of resources might be the lack of volunteers (or staff), lack of funds, or shortage of time. It is one thing to say we make time for that which matters most to us. However, in daily living, no one has the time they desire. Again, life in congregations (as in life outside of congregations) is often constrained by competing values. Congregational activities compete for not only focus but also resources like funds and time, too.

You may have found that revelation doesn't turn into action because there simply aren't the leaders needed to move the spark of the idea into energy for action. This is a different challenge than having enough volunteers. Having the right *leader* is its own category. It is a wise pastor (or board) that decides to hold off taking on something new until a capable leader is identified.

Sometimes implementation stalls because there is lack of alignment between the endeavor and the overarching purpose of the congregation. Not every flash of insight discloses the soul of a faith community. For example, a certain suburban congregation received a grant to fund a new community ministry. Early in the project, the board discerned that while the congregation was devoted to the community, it wasn't devoted to more assessments and fund-raising. So, the board voted to return the grant. They chose to spend more time improving a project they already were doing: a weekly identification ministry that helped people get their personal documentation in order. One way to cast this change would be to say that the congregation failed to take a risk. More accurately, I think, the leaders learned more about what they valued. Such knowledge led to a difficult decision. Yet, it was a decision acquired by experience—a learning experience.

Your congregation doesn't just do a program. Even if it is a program you've done many times before—a mission trip, a homecoming—your congregation is always learning how to do this specific incarnation of the event. The learning framework for congregational endeavors suggests that nothing is simply repeated. Every meaningful event is both a taking on of activities and a taking on of learning how to do the specific activity given the present reality. Every year the Vacation Bible School is different in some way. One moment in time is different from another and requires new applied knowledge of leaders.

MAKING IT WORK

There are more helpers—that is, there are more outside resources—available to help you dream than there are to help you implement. Yet, attention to specific duties can keep you moving ahead. Creating a task list is essential. The list is almost always long (see below). To do something well requires consideration of almost all of these elements. It is best to know ahead of time all the work that is needed.

These elements include

- being clear about your purpose,
- defining roles and functions,
- finding the right people to do the work,
- using well-matched outside resources as guiding counsel,
- establishing a project planning chart,
- creating a checklist of activities,
- creating a timeline,
- forming a budget,
- forming a communication plan, and
- planning to evaluate.

The first step of moving an idea from dream to reality is to be clear what that reality is. Reality is your friend. Just as clearly defining the challenge is a significant first step to starting a learning journey, refining exactly what is to be done is key to taking on and implementing the new project. New projects deserve purpose statements. Such statements need to be aligned with the overall mission of the congregation. A purpose statement is a single sentence (at most two) that states why this new endeavor is essential.

For the parenting program that Essie led, this was the purpose statement: "We want parents to take control of their family responsibilities so that their children are safe and growing." Such a statement was congruent with the congregation's mission statement: "We are a family of faith making Jesus Christ a way of life." This congregation valued family as both a biological construct and as a communal actuality consisting of relationships beyond biology. For this congregation, the phrase "making Jesus Christ a way of life" referred not only to practicing what was preached, but also to the notion that faith connects to experience beyond church things. Faith relates to everyday experience including vocation, health, marriage, and, in this instance, parenting.

Essie started the Parenting Group (that's what she called the program) by creating a team. She recruited three people to be present at the meetings. They helped teach the curriculum. They did operational tasks. It was clear that Essie was the leader. It was also clear that this was not a solo flight for her.

However, just as taking on a new endeavor requires a functioning team, such work also requires a high quality leader (as noted above). This congregation was blessed to have a leader like Essie who was both passionate about the program and highly capable as a leader. The taking on aspect of a learning journey is rigorous work. Essie was willing to do the sometimes mundane (but taxing) work of program management (will there be snacks?). She recruited participants tirelessly. She contacted *all* the parents in the congregation and invited to them to attend programs. She didn't do this just once; she did this repeatedly. Essie called leaders of nonprofits. She called judges. She called neighbors. She called school counselors and teachers. She called pastors from other congregations. She called foster parents and grandparents. Even if years later people have forgotten the content of the parenting curriculum, they remember Essie as someone who *cared* about them. Accomplishing something new in your congregation requires a leader who is willing to work overtime.

The next step is to assign roles and functions. The roles and functions need to be clear on both an individual level and on an organizational level. What team or committee will be responsible for the effort? What group does this team report to? And how often? Who will lead the work? Though this was not the case with Essie, it is not unusual to find that those who dreamed of the new endeavor may not be the best people suited to carry out the endeavor.

For her work, Essie established a program-planning chart. You can create a chart that works best for you. But don't go without such a worksheet. A program-planning chart provides visible feedback about what is getting done and what needs attention.

Similarly, people who are gifted at making an idea a reality often create checklists of various tasks. The program-planning chart captures the overall trajectory of the project. The checklist divides the elements of the planning chart into smaller steps. I know one lay leader who made a checklist template for her congregation that could be adapted for every event hosted by the church. The board looked over the checklist one meeting and promptly voted to make its usage mandatory for everyone leading a program.

A timeline needs to be established. The riskier the project the more the timeline needs to be broken down into smaller segments. Work backward from an ending point or a culmination point. Everything in creation is bounded in time. Make a macro and a micro timeline. That is, if you are working on a program (like the Parenting Group), create a schedule for all the activities that will produce the events (that's macro), and make an agenda for each singular event, too (that's micro).

Consistent with the learning-journey model, Essie sought outside resources to construct the formal curriculum of the program. The congregation budgeted for and distributed a workbook called *The Parent's Handbook: Systematic Training for Effective Parenting.*[5] Additionally, Essie called on local pastoral counselors to facilitate groups.

Ascertain a budget. Money does matter. A prerequisite for establishing a budget is coming to agreement on how the endeavor will be funded. List expected expenditures. Where will funds come from? How much can be spent for what? Start with an overall amount and then break down expenditures into into line items. Who has responsibility to request payments? How will this project be sustainable if it runs for more than one program year?

New programs should yield *results* and *impact*. In her book *Projects That Matter*, Kathleen Cahalan differentiates between these two evaluative terms.[6] Results are often numbers: the number of people involved, the number of events held, the number of resources used, and the budget needed. Impact, according to Cahalan, "is a way of talking about how the project activities affect people, particularly the people who face the problem need, question, or opportunity. Impact includes behavior and attitude change."[7]

Constant, creative communication strengthens the chance of success for a new endeavor. Essie was tireless in sharing what she was learning with the church board. She made announcements on Sunday morning. She wrote newsletter articles about what was being learned. She wrote follow-up notes to participants. She talked to everyone who would listen about the Parenting Group. She asked for ideas about topics and speakers.

Taking On

Overarching Challenge:

....
....

Idea Or Program:

....
....

Why (Goal):

....
....
....

What (Activities):

....
....
....

Who (is Responsible):

....
....
....

Budget:

....
....
....

Time Line:

....
....

Figure 7.1.

When Essie developed a plan for the Parenting Group, the implementation elements noted above were included. She went to work on timelines, budgets, checklists, and much more. For her, it was all about action steps.

Just as the program was about systematic parenting, so her leadership was about the systematic administration of the program.

LIFE, LEARNING, AND YOUR CONGREGATION

Recall that earlier three realms of congregational learning were identified: religious, life practice, and organizational. The Parenting Group is an example where all three realms were in play. However, the life practice of parenting was primary. What would it be like for more congregations to function as a curator of resources that help people live more fully into their personal hopes and dreams? There are resource centers that help congregations with their challenges and opportunities. What if congregations functioned as resource centers to help members with *their* challenges and opportunities? In other words, what if congregational learning was not just about building the institutional capacity of the congregation, but also about lifting the life capacity of those touched by the congregation?

Of course, an effective congregation is attentive to operations. It will learn to make sound decisions in an orderly way. Bills will be paid on time. Money matters will be managed with integrity and transparency. Each staff person will know his or her primary role and function. Building maintenance challenges will be handled without a sense of crisis. Effective congregations are run well.

Healthy congregations also attend deeply to spiritual matters. After all, this is what distinguishes congregations from other social communities. Such congregations have multiple ways for congregants to explore, define, and ultimately live out their relationship with God. Worship, study of scripture, prayer, and acts of service are designed to strengthen participants' relationship with the Creator.

Ultimately, congregations that are making a beautiful and positive difference help people live more effectively among the horizontal realities of life: family, community, money, work, volunteering, and much more. Life isn't easy. Many of us face challenges that confound us, about which we feel ill-equipped. Some of the most vibrant congregations are ones that help people navigate *life* with greater skill and creativity. The focus on God is what often differentiates a congregation from other organizations; congregations that apply that God attention to improving life are ones that often feel the most vital.

Picture a congregation structured to support members in finding conversation partners who will help them live out their God-inspired mission as it relates to their family (this is what the Parenting Group supported), their vocation, and their support of the common good beyond the congregation.

Many congregations work on matching their members with volunteer opportunities. There is endless need for congregations to fill volunteer positions such as greeters, coffee hour hosts, nursery attendants, and so forth. Such efforts often include completion of member talent forms and then data entry of the information into the church membership database. Leaders will advertise matching individuals with tasks as "people living out their calling." After all, it doesn't matter if your congregation is large or small, there is a need to recruit, train, and encourage members to help with the never-ending list of responsibilities.

What would it mean for congregations to be a resource center for people's lives, not just another organization needing, pleading for volunteers? A congregation of any size can take on the higher purpose of helping people increase their personal impact regarding life endeavors.

I think it is possible for a congregation to be a resource for its members' focus on serving God's world. In such a setting, a clergyperson would, as noted in chapter 2, add the role of *curate* to his or her role of preacher, teacher, and leader.

The word *curation* (derived from *curate*) has been applied to those who host websites that gather resources about specific subjects. Think Pinterest. There are many websites that display blogs and other forms of information about medical conditions, hobbies, social services, restaurants, professions, and more. In these cases, the act of curation, the gathering and vetting of resources, is helpful to those seeking more information about these subjects. The best of these websites do more than provide data; they provide information and Internet-mediated relationships that improve life.

What would it look like for the congregation to be curated space about life? Congregations are sanctuaries of knowledge. A congregation could become a curated public space for any number of life interests. Such a stance would acknowledge the congregation as an essential social network, an organic assembly—yes, a family of faith. Congregational focus on learning and life practice would require curates who are adept at social networking in terms of nurturing relationships: introducing people to others who care about similar interests. It would require listening to parishioners in a way that attunes to what they most care about and what they most want help with.

Congregational leaders, clergy and laity alike, know a lot about life. They may not be experts about every subject, but they often know who to talk to, what to read, and where to go to learn more about any number of life issues. How might your congregation harness this knowledge for the good of more people? To the extent you are able, you will be shaping your congregation into a learning community for the good of one another and for the sake of God's good world.

Let's return to Essie, the leader of the Parenting Group. She once wrote about her own mother's advice, "'When you're in doubt or trouble, pray every step of the way,' she advised me. 'Then you won't think of fear. Prayer will take you where you need to go.'"[8] Family and faith are dearly important to Essie. She wants to share what she has learned just as her mother had for her. She wants the congregation to be the host of that learning. And she knows that new activities don't just happen in a faith community like turning on your computer and seeing the screen come to life. Taking on new activities means checklists, timelines, budgets; many phone calls, e-mails and texts, planning charts, change in plans, and much more. *Someone* has to make sure these things happen.

Right now, watch Essie in front of one hundred people wanting to learn something new about being a parent. She knows them all by name. She didn't sleep last night thinking about whether there would be enough food. Had she remembered to voucher the honorariums? But if you are in this group when she says to everyone gathered, "I've been expecting you," you know this "something new" isn't just any old thing. Something essential to who you are is about to be disclosed; something worth knowing is about to be shared. This is about life. And learning.

LETTING GO

When a congregation takes on a new endeavor it almost always has to let go of something else. Your congregation has limited time. Your congregation does not have unlimited resources. Acknowledgment of limits isn't meant to hinder; it allows for careful attention to the new thing taking form.

When it is time for a congregation to move ahead with a new project, it is important for the congregational leaders to take inventory of other activities. Is there something that has run its course? Is there a program that needs to be put on hold? Is there a new idea that can wait its turn?

Letting go is part of taking on. Letting go is the action of releasing something in the congregation in order to allow space for the new. This dynamic is true no matter the size of the congregation. We might assume that a larger, growing congregation is able to take on more activities. This may be true for a time. Eventually any human community will experience the inadequacy of doing too much. If something is worth doing well, then something else is worth not doing. We often don't know we've taken on too much until we've taken on too much.

In the stories of congregations that have accomplished new things a consistent element emerged. When a congregation took on something new it almost always stopped doing something else.

A mission team decides to support a local food pantry. At the same time, they choose to not host the Gideon's anymore. A youth pastor makes a commitment to visit first-year college students. She gives up going to the monthly ministerial meeting. The worship team adds video to accompany the sermon. For a season they stop writing new choruses for worship.

Everything has a life cycle. The very new program you are learning to implement right now will not last forever. Congregational life mirrors the rest of life. We work hard to establish new routines, to learn new habits, to start new initiatives. Someday, these things will have run their course. They will no longer serve us well. It is as if we humans eventually acquire an immunity to almost everything, even to that which is good. One of the lessons of a learning congregation is that nothing lasts forever. Even the programs we value and that represent tradition are temporal and in time will give way to new programs and practices.

Sometimes the letting go has emotional dynamics. Lead your congregation to the needed renovation of your sanctuary and you will hear people talking about how much they miss the red carpet. At risk is more than aesthetic differences. This is about attachments.

Early in life we become attached to objects. The objects include our parents.[9] They include items at home, our pillow, our blanket. Objects are crucial to how we learn to accept support, express our needs, and have our needs met. It is natural that as we grow older we relate to certain objects as expressions of the Divine. As adults, our attachments are to a variety of objects—that is, people, things, activities, places, memories, and so forth. In a congregation, you can anticipate that almost any object holds meaning for someone. You can assume that the loss of any object will create an affective response in some person.

The range of affective responses include sadness, fear, uncertainty, anger, or sometimes free-floating anxiety. The changes, or letting go, will feel like danger to some. This is more than not liking change. We become attached to walls, pews, crosses, arks, tables, pulpits, Bibles, and much more because over time they become external representations of the internal trust that we need to carry within us to function as developing adults in a complex world. Mature people don't somehow outgrow the need for such attachments. In fact, mature people, high-functioning people, have ably internalized a diverse constellation of attachments.

Move the cross to make room for the projector if you need to. But don't do it without knowing that you are moving an object that not only represents a salvific act for the community, but may also be a contemporary symbol of consolation for an individual—a consolation that may be the very thing that moves a person to address personal grief in brave ways.

Sometimes the letting go is cognitive. It involves letting go of an idea. That's what an early career pastor discovered when his congregation received a gift of $500,000. A former member who had long since moved to California gave the gift to the church in gratitude for the community that had cared so well for his mother. He was wealthy, having made more money than he had ever imagined working in Silicon Valley. Shortly after his mother died, the check arrived at the church. The pastor had always thought of money as the root of all evil. He admits he hadn't read 1 Timothy 6:10 closely. "I really didn't want to deal with it," he remembers. "It was like someone had given me a birthday gift I didn't want."

This pastor typed the search words "money and faith" into the Google search engine. He found an online articled titled "Money and Faith: William G. Enright and the Big American Taboo."[10] After he read the article he changed his thinking. "Money wasn't evil," he said. "It can be a way for God to get God's work done." He was now ready to start a conversation with his council about uses for the new fund. To get to this place the pastor let go of one idea about money to take on a new perspective about money.

If you have clearly defined the new challenge, explored resources and possibilities, been part of a group that has had a discovery that affirms the way forward, then don't let the challenges of letting go stop the forward movement of what you are trying to achieve. You may choose to slow down certain aspects of the project to let people adapt to that which is new, but if you have indeed been on a learning journey, trust the learning and keep moving ahead.

You and other leaders will want to find ways to acknowledge the discomfort that some are feeling or thinking. You will not want to, however, let emotionality override strategic decisions. There is a difference between acknowledging emotions and being moved off course by unregulated emotionality. You may think allowing people to express their unhappiness is cathartic—the pastoral thing to do. In reality, without boundaries such unregulated emotionality only delays resolution. Being overly concerned for those who are experiencing loss extends the time of negative emotions. Inadvertently, you are doing more harm by paying too much attention to the loss. You can acknowledge the trouble some might be having in letting go. You can listen; you can show empathy. Be curious. Yet know you can't solve or resolve the feelings for them.

Whether it is attachment to an object, or a negative emotion, or a way of thinking, implementing new activities in a congregation requires letting go as well as taking on. One helpful element of taking on and letting go is attention to rites of passage. We will now turn to the learning behaviors related to rites of passage.

RITES OF PASSAGE

There is a positive correlation between congregations that learn effectively and their attention to *rites of passages*. There are many different, complex theological and sociological definitions of "rites of passages." For the sake of our work I want to simplify it like this: *A rite of passage is a meaningful experience, real or emblematic, that signifies a change in life situation that is significant to the person or community experiencing the change.*

For a congregation, a rite of passage might involve a change for the community of faith as a whole—like welcoming a new pastor. Moving to a new site is a rite of passage. For individuals or households within the congregation, a rite of passage involves something that may be sacramental (a baptism) or some other important life event like birth, a new job, marriage, moving, death, and so forth.

It is important for a congregation that is gaining capacity to do new and sometimes challenging things to pay attention to both kinds of rites—those experienced by the whole congregation and those specific to the experience of individuals.

Let's start with the latter. When new learning is taking place it is important for congregations to pay attention to tender and transitional moments of existence: birth, graduation, wedding, divorce, illness, recovery, and death. Paying attention to such threshold moments of life has its own intrinsic value—even if the threshold moments do not have a direct connection to a particular learning journey.

You may have experienced a heightened sense of reality recovering after surgery. You may have found reality particularly intense when sending a child off to school. There is much to learn from these experiences. Illness may teach you to be grateful for life. Or it might teach you to be more careful about how you take care of your body. Or you may feel sad or even angry. Leaving a child at college for the first time might teach that time is fleeting. (It really does seem like yesterday that she was saying "daddy" for the first time.)

If your congregation can find ways to honor these tender and transitional moments, people will be less alone during such moments. Recognizing transitional experiences builds the capacity for individuals and the community to learn from such moments. This is because the learning doesn't happen only because of the experience. Learning happens because of the connections between people in the midst of such experiences. Acknowledging, testifying to, holding up such liminal experiences makes these sometimes complicated transitions more manageable. The congregation becomes a place that makes complex events safer, and if not safe, more tolerable. In this way your congregation as a learning organization is a secure environment for learning to take place. Your congregation is a school teaching about the transience of life. And your congregation becomes more resilient regarding the learning required in the organizational and overtly religious realms of life together. In other words, general attention to rites of passages strengthens learning about any number of related and even unrelated congregational endeavors.

As a learning community your congregation can find ways to lift up such transitional experiences. This can occur in simple ways. One congregation has a large dinner bell hanging from a wall in the fellowship hall. Anyone can ring the bell to get the attention of those gathered. On this day, it is clear the purpose of the announcements isn't to remind people when the next committee night is going to be or who is cutting the grass on the church lawn that week. The announcements, on this day, are all about life. Marigold's ninety-fifth birthday is this week. The Sampsons are bringing their baby home from the hospital. Jack is flying to Honduras with the medical supplies for the village.

A leader who is learning to take on a new endeavor will listen for transitional moments between the story lines of people's lives. Those experiencing transitions are learning. Such learning by individuals can and should receive attention. In addition to being the right thing to do, such attention builds the ability for a congregation to view learning as part of its culture.

When your congregation is learning something new, reflect on new developments happening in your life. There very well could be a synchronistic parallel between something happening in your life and something you are trying to do with your congregation. This isn't magical thinking. This is reality shaped by sacred connections of which we aren't always conscious. Think back to the earlier chapter where Mark is attending to his grandmother while at the same time thinking about care for older adults in his congregation. Such parallels are signals that you and perhaps your congregation are ready to pay special attention to the subject. Rites of passage focus our attention in this way.

So, some rites of passages are embedded in the life-practice realm of a congregant's experience. Other rites are solidly rooted in the community life of the congregation. Many congregations hold sacramental rites of passages. Baptism is such a rite. So is anointing with oil at times of illness or in preparation for death. Congregations also hold rites that are unique to their setting. Many congregations celebrate anniversaries of being established. Many congregations have annual festivals. Such markings of time carry with them rites that have been established over the years.

It is possible for a rite like baptism to be a shallow experience. It can be something that occurs to serve a family expectation (my mother won't be quiet about this until we call the church and get it scheduled). A rite can use materials or words that no longer hold meaning (why would the priest rub oil on grandpa?). However, when the rite expresses meaning congruent with the experience being represented it reinforces the learning that is taking place. Infant baptism (practiced in many, but not all, Christian congregations) can indeed signal parental trust in the Creator and the community—not just the parents' own wiles. Or, it can signal, perhaps more truthfully, the parents' desire to learn to trust more in the Creator and the community of faith. Rites represent learning. Ask: What is the meaning of this rite of passage? Then, reframe the answer to that question into a statement of what is being learned.

What is the relationship between such rites and taking on and letting go? Congregational rites are a way to publicly acknowledge change and all its accompanying, ambivalent thoughts and feelings. If you are working on implementing a new endeavor for your congregation and the team with responsibility for implementation is stuck, consider if there is some ritual or symbolic activity that you could encourage. You are likely to be pleased that participation in such activity releases new energy.

THE SACRED ART OF IMPLEMENTATION

You might be tempted to think of the implementation of a new endeavor as simply tactical work. It is in many ways. Taking on a new project after careful exploration requires concrete thinking. It benefits from developing timelines, checklists, and budgets. There is a levelheaded, businesslike element to executing a new program.

There is also something spiritually gratifyingly about pulling off a new project. You are giving voice and motion to an epiphany, a moment of discovery. You are helping a community do something new—that is, you are creating with God. You are attending to the variety of thoughts and feelings people have about taking on something new and letting go of something that has run its course of usefulness.

Yes, implementation of a new idea involves practical wisdom.[11] You are thinking through the right way to do the right thing at the right time. In addition, don't lose sight that action itself is to be revered. This is practical and *holy* work. On certain days, Martha, not Mary, deserves her due (Luke 10:38–42).

One of the learning behaviors of a learning congregation is the ability to use words, to use conversation, to move ideas ahead. You learn to succinctly express a challenge; you learn to talk about lots of ideas during the exploration phase. You learn to be better storytellers. In terms of conversation while taking on this new thing, you want your words to convey a bias for action. The time has passed for brainstorming new activities. Some congregations are disposed to talking certain ideas to death. If your congregation is experiencing this trait, you will appreciate leaders who persistently ask, "What's our next step?" while taking on a new project. While taking the Parenting Group to reality, Essie spent far more time on the phone recruiting participants than she did debating the value of certain parenting research or wondering if a Couples Group might have been a better idea.

What was that idea that started some time ago? What have you learned since? What new thing is now taking shape? The answers to these questions include lessons learned. And lessons learned are sacred evidence of God's presence with you; a presence not standing still but walking a road not fully mapped or realized. Until now.

You know you are experiencing the taking on and letting go phase of a learning journey when the following occur:

- You are creating a checklist of actions steps.
- Someone is reporting to a team, committee, or board a timeline, roles for individuals, and budget requests.
- A person shares with you that they are upset that something they care about is coming to an end.
- You are talking with another person about a rite of passage that reflects the new project you are working on.
- Some skill or interest you have applied to another realm of your life is of good use to the project you are putting into effect.

Questions to ask when you are moving through the experience of taking on and letting go include the following:

- Who are the right people to make this happen?
- What practical considerations are there to making this excellent and not just another thing we do?
- What is the congregation going to let go of?
- How can we shape this new activity so that it bolsters our religious growth, life skills, and the health of our congregation?
- What rites of passages mirror what we are trying to do?
- How do we pay just enough attention to the discomfort this is causing?

Things you can do when in the midst of taking on and letting go include the following:

- Create a checklist of "to do" tasks.
- Create and fill out a program-planning chart including roles and function, timeline, budget, results and impact, and so forth.
- If you have defined your challenge, explored resources, and interpreted moments of insight, keep your focus now on implementation.
- Create conversations that represent a bias for action.

Chapter Eight

Validation

Celebrating Your Accomplishments

To learn new things your congregation needs *validation*. People need to know their efforts are valued; their efforts should not be minimized. You don't want those who are part of new endeavors to feel invisible. Accomplishments should not be hidden. They need to be lifted up in plain sight.

The first congregation I served, Bethlehem Presbyterian Church, had a hymn sing the first Sunday of every month. Bob Williamson led the hymns during worship. He started each with his favorite song. It was "Love Lifted Me," lyrics by James Rowe and music by Howard Smith. If you know the hymn, you have heard the rolling gospel style of the music. The lyrics begin with presumably Peter sinking while walking on the water. "I was sinking deep in sin, far from the peaceful shore." Then Jesus's gospel power holds him up, raises him up. Hence the refrain: "Love lifted me, Love lifted me, When nothing else could help, Love lifted me." God saves. God redeems. God *validates* our imperfect efforts. Our efforts are recognized. Our efforts are legitimate. They are worthy even if they are imperfect. The time and energy, the prayer and desire offered are worthy of recognition. Such recognition provides staying power for the long journey of a project.

Story after story of vibrant congregations include experiences of validation. Validation is the affirmation of a person and his or her contribution. This involves recognition. It often involves blessing, celebration, and testimony. The result is as if love has lifted the recipient of validation.

Validation reveals a good previously hidden. The act of validation involves the recognition of a benefit that had previously been veiled. Remember Arthur Miller's classic play *Death of a Salesman*. Willy Lowman is the salesman. He is lost. Or he has lost a sense of self-respect. Dignity is lacking.

127

His wife doesn't know how to support him. How could she know? In act 1
she comments:

> I don't say he's a great man. Willy Loman never made a lot of money. His
> name was never in the paper. He's not the finest character that ever lived. But
> he's a human being, and a terrible thing is happening to him. So attention must
> be paid. He'd not to be allowed to fall into his grave like an old dog. Attention,
> attention must finally be paid to such a person. [1]

The people in your congregation deserve more recognition than Willy
Loman received. It is not easy working on a new endeavor. There are dead-
lines to meet, complaints coming their way, disappointments to manage,
frustrations to endure. If the project leader is a volunteer, there is typically no
pay. Individuals in your congregation, clergy and laity alike, deserve support.
They should have their efforts validated.

Your congregation gains strength when its efforts are lifted up and seen as
making a difference. Community affirmation keeps the soul of your congregation willing to take on the learning that is needed to accomplish new
things. Without such validation the church slips into an aura of invisibility.
Your work becomes withdrawn, hidden from sight. The angel of your congregation could feel that important activities matter to no one. If so, congregants carry an uneasy sense that what they hold as significant is not only met
with indifference, but is essentially unnoticed by others.

Have you ever served an invisible church? The Rev. Lori Bievenour has.
For years St. Peter's was known as the church across from McDonald's.
Ultimately, the identification with McDonald's just wasn't powerful enough
to feed a spiritual journey. *St. Peter's, that's your congregation, now where
are you in town?*

So, Lori wants St. Peter's Church to become *uninvisible.* That's the word
she uses. A friend asks Lori, "Don't you mean visible?" Lori says, "No, I
really mean uninvisible, because we're really good at being invisible. Becoming uninvisible is fundamentally different from simply becoming visible."

One of St. Peter's efforts is to establish a native habitat on its grounds.
The idea isn't borrowed from a book or a blog. It develops out of real life.
Members observe that there is too much grass to cut. The volunteers don't
have to cut the grass themselves; they contract the work. Yet, they don't like
paying the bills for lawn care. It is expensive.

There is more than the desire to save money. Several leaders care not only
about the church grounds, but also about the health of our blue planet.
Among members there is a wish to be a green congregation—a congregation
that addresses issues of environmental stewardship. They want to represent
gratefulness for God's creation.

Some people talk about the native habitat in terms of honoring creation. Others talk about it in terms of the amount of construction going on around them and the resulting lack of green space available to families. Others view the habitat as a way to provide a nature sanctuary for children. The presence of a native habitat would support a preschool curriculum that invites children to think about how and where they see God in creation.

If you stand with Lori on the church property you will see a new landscape appearing (actually an old, native landscape). The turf grass is giving way to native plants. Look one way and you will see a rain garden. Look another way and you will see indigenous trees, bright green against the sky. Is that a butterfly? Yes it is. Butterflies like native habitats more than manicured lawns. They're present at St. Peter's.

It hasn't been easy for St. Peter's to establish the native habitat. Like other learning journeys, learning to create the native habitat involved several challenges. Whether the challenge had to do with saving money, taking care of the earth, or becoming uninvisible, the congregation experienced disappointments and discoveries along the way. Some people didn't understand the plan. ("So, what are we doing with the lawn?") For some of the volunteers this was their first time working on a native habitat. New skills had to be learned.

One aha moment came when volunteers looked to their right and saw it. It was a nest of newly moved-in, resident hawk bunnies. At this sight, people knew the project was heading in the right direction. The sighting was a validation of their efforts.

It also helped when the phone rang. The voice on the other end of the phone was informing Pastor Lori of a prize. Lori learned that St. Peter's Church had won an award of $1,000. What Lori learned was that Interfaith Power and Light had awarded St. Peter's United Church of Christ one of five top prizes in its annual Cool Congregations Challenge. "We used to be known as the church across from McDonald's," Lori says. "Now we are the church with the native habitat."

Lori and the rest of the congregation received the award humbly. They received it gratefully. They certainly didn't want to accept the award as some deserved honor that set them apart from the good work many other congregations were doing. Yet, the affirmation showed that *someone* had paid attention to their efforts.

When your congregation is well on its way through a new project and the project is going well, there will be moments of validation that come your way. When such affirmations arrive, whether internal or external, celebrate! Give thanks that the potential that was once hidden is now visible.

CELEBRATE

Celebration is a healthy response to accomplishment. Much of congregation life exists in the space between complaining and commitment. Celebration can help tilt that space toward deeper commitment and fewer complaints. Robert Kegan and Lisa Lahey have observed that our complaints reveal our commitments.[2] We wouldn't complain if we didn't care. Sometimes, though, complaining can become the major chord. This isn't healthy for an individual; it isn't healthy for a congregation; it isn't healthy for a community. Complaining drains energy. If too pervasive, complaint drains commitment from even the most gifted congregational leaders. Faultfinding gets in the way of learning.

A friend of mine tells the story of a clergyperson who wanted to hold a meeting to address simmering conflict in the congregation. It was a meeting where people could air their grievances. Complaints would be welcome. My friend listened to his clergy friend's plans and then asked, "So, why would you want to hurt your people this way?" Conflict resolution is a good, though tricky, thing. Simply airing complaints is harmful.

Celebration is positive energy. It strengthens commitment. I recall listening to a Fred Craddock sermon given at an annual Montreat Worship Conference. Craddock noted all the wonderful things he was observing at the event. There was much to affirm, much to validate, much to celebrate. He commented that the church just doesn't celebrate enough. "There should be more rejoicing in the church," said Craddock.

Think of Philippians 4:4: "Rejoice in the Lord always; again I will say, Rejoice." Paul is responding to the generosity of others. Inside he feels gratitude. Paul expresses his gratitude outwardly with words. The last chapter of Philippians is a beautiful model of a thank you note. "You Philippians indeed know that in the early days of the gospel, when I left Macedonia, no church shared with me in the matter of giving and receiving, except you alone" (Phil. 4:15).

Paul's gratitude then leads to exhortation. His exhortation names actions, which are a series of validations: "Finally, beloved, whatever is true, whatever is honorable, whatever is just, whatever is pure, whatever is pleasing, whatever is commendable, if there is any excellence and if there is anything worthy of praise, think about these things" (Phil. 4:8).

The transliteration for the word "think" in the Greek text is *logizomai*. This denotes more than casual thought. It denotes a conclusion, a reckoning, a decision that immediately precedes an action. To think about gratitude leads to an action and that action is celebration.

How does your congregation celebrate? A precursor to answering this question is to think about the wonderful things that happen in your congregation. Put aside for a moment the disappointment. Dwell beyond the understandable yet ultimately unhelpful complaints. Think of the positive accomplishments of your community of faith. One week I asked congregational leaders with whom I worked to name experiences worth celebrating. Of the ten clergy asked not one paused. They swiftly answered:

- We had 105 kids at Vacation Bible School. Twenty more than last year.
- A month ago we streamed our first sermon live over the Internet.
- We took a freewill offering for our project with the school and raised more than $1,000.
- We had a surprise party for Mrs. Behymer celebrating her ninety-fifth birthday.
- I heard news that I received a clergy renewal grant.
- Our youth choir safely returned from their Scotland tour.
- Last month, five of our members went to Kenya and worked at a medical mission.
- The board voted to implement a year with the Bible emphasis.
- Just this week we voted not to move, but to stay in the neighborhood where we are getting to know everyone by name.
- This fall our new associate pastor arrives. We've never had more than one clergyperson.
- In a month we will give out small grants to young social entrepreneurs.

Each of these accomplishments represents a nodal point, if not a culmination of work. These accomplishments invite celebration. They are true, honorable, just, pure, pleasing, and commendable things. They are worthy of celebration. Paul would sing, "Rejoice and again I say 'Rejoice.'" Think about these things. Such thoughts will lead you to celebrate.

So, how does your congregation celebrate? Some celebrations begin because of affirmations from beyond, as in the case of St. Peter's and the award they received for their natural habitat. Some celebrations begin from within as in honoring a clergyperson for ten years of service.

Celebrations occur in congregations because clergy and laity have learned the importance of marking accomplishments. The accomplishment could be reaching a capital campaign goal, attaining a new threshold in worship attendance, finishing a building project, or hosting a prayer vigil for the city.

Celebrate people. Some of us are hesitant to lift up one person at the risk of ignoring another. However, there are those in your congregation who have shown commitment beyond reasonable expectations. Such commitment should be commended. In your congregation many would welcome the opportunity to say "thank you" to a longtime Sunday School teacher, a missionary who is visiting, a former pastor who is preaching.

Celebrations are performative. Announcing a celebration, in a way, performs the very act of celebrating. It gives the community something special to anticipate. The anticipation creates good feelings. Creating a celebration seals joy, gratitude, hope, cheerfulness, kindness, confidence, and many other positive emotions in the congregation.

What constitutes a celebration? Congregational celebrations include various combinations of the following:

- food
- fellowship
- thank yous, spoken and handwritten
- gifts
- music
- multimedia presentations
- dance
- other forms of art
- important people from the past
- people from beyond the immediate congregational community
- symbols of faith
- personal testimony
- humor
- proclamations
- stories
- games

As an exercise, think of something you'd like to celebrate in your congregation. Now, choose three of the elements noted above. Design a celebration using those three elements. Repeat the process choosing another achievement and three different elements. What kind of a celebration is coming to mind? You will want to find ways natural to your faith community to celebrate accomplishments.

In a small-town church, twelve members and two clergy finished an eight-month-long study of God and poverty. They read the Gospel of Matthew. They discussed the book *Toxic Charity* by Robert Lupton.[3] The group went on a field trip to Chicago, spending a week working with a Christian nonprofit that supports the homeless. During Lent the individuals gave a prodigal amount of money away while spending close to nothing on themselves. When the eight months passed they decided to celebrate. The celebration wasn't about their accomplishment. The group had made a short video depicting the special people they had met. The study group wanted to introduce these special people, via the video, to others. They invited the community to a cookout ("we had an indoor cookout in our church basement"). Fifty people assembled to mark the end of the class. Bread was broken—or more accurately, pulled pork was shared. A discussion took place. At the end everyone sang an old Charles Albert Tindley hymn titled "We'll Understand It Better By and By."

> We are often destitute
> of the things that life demands,
> want of food and want of shelter,
> thirsty hills and barren lands;
> we are trusting in the Lord,
> and according to God's word,
> we will understand it better by and by

Even though the subject they had been studying was difficult, those at the gathering felt close to one another and to God. They reported a commitment to continue learning about poverty—not as something distant and theoretical, but as something occurring far too frequently to people with names, faces, and families.

Think about the good things happening in your congregation and rejoice in the Lord.

VALIDATION AND THE ART OF CONVERSATION

A learning congregation validates good work through not only celebration, but also conversation. Spoken words of affirmation serve to make even more real the good news that exists. One pastor whose congregation has repeatedly accomplished new things says that his mentor told him, "Always highlight the good over and over and over and over and over again." The pastor says, "When my mentor got to the fourth 'over' I told him, 'I get it.'"

Dr. John Gottman has studied marriage. He has discovered a high-accuracy indicator of which marriages will last. He knows that in stable, vibrant marriages, couples will share five affirmations for every one complaint. In contrast, marriages headed to divorce offer fewer than one positive comment for every single negative remark.[4]

Congregational learning is not the same as a marriage relationship. However, the information is relevant. Positive regard builds connection. Connection strengthens the capacity to explore a new challenge, to overcome disappointment and be open to moments of insight. Spoken validations produce positive emotions. Positive emotions indicate that learning and growth have occurred. All of this is to say that the disposition of your congregation influences its capacity to learn to do new things.

As a congregational leader, consider the reality that your congregation's accomplishments are connected to your ability to communicate the simple (or not so simple) reality that you *like* the congregation. Despite your congregation's quirks, despite its maladaptations, defenses, and failures to live up to its values, consistently communicate your enjoyment of those in the community of faith. These are people you appreciate.

BLESSING

One way to communicate your appreciation of your faith community is to be generous with words of blessing. Recall the blessing remembered in Numbers 6:24–26:

> The Lord bless you and keep you;
> the Lord make his face shine upon
>   you, and be gracious to you;
> the Lord lift up his countenance
> upon you, and give you peace.

God is speaking to Moses. The blessing isn't meant exclusively for Moses. God wants Moses to share these words with others—specifically Aaron and his sons. God blesses. Yet, based on this text, we are instructed by God to bless others. Would that it be so that our congregations could be the voice of God blessing others. As a congregational leader you can be an exemplar of blessings.

Blessings represent numinous moments. These include times in congregational life when learning is apparent, when an accomplishment comes into plain view, when a revelation has become part of the rhythm of communal life.

Yet, blessings don't have to wait until explicitly holy moments. Blessings can be voiced in the presence of the mundane. This would include affirmations at mealtime, during weekly routines, on the occasion of anniversaries and such. Rabbi Lawrence Hoffman asserts that blessings unite that which we often treat as oppositions. Hoffman notes that we often view life as "either at work or at play, on vacation or on the job, in school or at recess."[5] Words of blessings signal to a congregation that God is active throughout all seasons of life. A natural habitat can represent the work of God and so can Sunday liturgy in the sanctuary.

One pastor gathers the children at the front of the sanctuary every week, not for a lesson on scripture, but to offer a blessing to every young person present. She asks each child to name one important thing that had happened to them during the past week. The pastor then forms a blessing using the responses the congregation has just overheard. "William, you are blessed to have your grandparents visiting this week." "Jennifer, you are beloved by God whether you make the team or not." Blessings seal an important reality: God is present in all aspects of our life.

Additionally, the act of blessing creates positive attachment between the speaker and the recipient. Blessings reinforce any number of life lessons, not the least of which is that relationships are the material of learning. Whether the congregational learning has to do with the mundane or the explicitly spiritual, or with organizational life or religious learning, the relationship between the one offering the blessing and the one receiving the blessing is what creates the opportunity space for learning.

When sharing a blessing do not speak in generalities. Whether you are speaking to an individual, a team, or the entire congregation, be specific. Three things make a blessing powerful: First, a blessing should validate something that is true about the relationship between God and the person (or community). For example when the pastor noted above blesses children, she often says that "no one can separate you from Christ's love." Second, a blessing can validate a positive behavior ("we would never have fed 150 hungry people without your determination"). Third, a blessing can include a metaphor or image that reinforces and elaborates on the behavior being affirmed. Authors John Trent and Gary Smalley emphasize the importance of creating a word picture when offering a blessing. This word picture can express a special future in specific language.[6] A pastor speaks to Mrs. Behymer on her birthday: "God will bless your family tree, extending to the sky with branches touching the firmament. Years from now new limbs will still be growing from roots you planted."

A pastor was asked to create a prayer for the dedication of the new building for the congregation's counseling center. It had not been an easy project. At first there was the disappointment that the building was going to cost more than expected. The conceptual drawings were perhaps too conceptual! Then there was the disappointment that the capital campaign raised 20 percent less than the goal. Though there was every indication that the congregation was going to be just fine financially, there was still wilderness grumbling about the cost. On the night before the dedication, the pastor found a prayer in a prayer book that was for the dedication of a facility. Yet, when he sat still with the prayer the night before the dedication he found that "it felt like I was praying for just any building, not the one we had dreamed about and worked so hard for the past three years." So, he woke up early the next morning and drove to the building. He walked through the halls. He imagined the people whose lives were going to be supported by work that took place there. He imagined a young person with depression finding hope that he might feel better. He pictured an older woman discovering a way forward from the loss of her husband of fifty years. The words started coming to him. He wrote a dozen short blessings. For the reception area he wrote, "May our hospitality bless every person who walks through these doors. May there be courage to address difficult things well. May this place become like a light in the shadows guiding one and all to a new horizon abundant with stars of hope." For the room of a therapist who works primarily with young children he wrote, "May each child know of God's eternal love that nothing can stop.

May the struggles of childhood be replaced with numerous possibilities for each person to grow to the full stature that God intends."

The pastor closed the service of dedication with the Aaronic blessing:

> The Lord bless you and keep you;
> the Lord make his face shine upon
>   you, and be gracious to you;
> the Lord lift up his countenance
> upon you, and give you peace. (Num. 6: 24–26)

At the end of the dedication, no one was concerned that the church had spent too much money on the building. They stood at the threshold of their new building. People could feel, at least for a moment, a buoyancy that represented the role positive emotions serve in human development. In listening to the stories of congregations that accomplish new things there is often a moment where the accomplishment is brought out beyond closed doors (no longer invisible) and into the sunshine. Such an occurrence is, itself, a blessing.

TESTIMONY

Blessings are a powerful form of validation. The same is true for testimony. A testimony is a public declaration of an important subject. Go back to the fourteenth century and the Latin word *testimonium* was translated as *commandment*. Think of the Ten Commandments as the Ten Testimonies. The commandments function as public declarations of God's ethics. Testimony also bears witness. To receive someone's testimony, to be on the listening end of someone's public declaration, is to pay attention to that person. To pay attention to another is to offer validation. It is possible to listen someone into greater depths of being.

Just as individuals need a witness, so your congregation needs a witness. When members of your congregation share testimonies of work completed, learning is sealed into the life of the community. The act of bearing witness fastens the learning to the community. The new knowledge, the new behavior becomes secure. Because it has been made public, it can be retrieved. It can be applied to new situations.

College Avenue United Methodist Church in Muncie, Indiana, had been working on intergenerational relationships. The pastor, the Rev. Lisa Schubert Nowling, recognized that one of the unique gifts of a congregation is that it provides opportunities for different ages of people to connect. Such connections provide reliable attachments that might not otherwise exist. A five year old might have a congregational grandparent. This is a good thing when her biological grandparents live four hundred miles away.

The Intergenerational Task Force at College Avenue United Methodist Church had been working hard. One of their challenges was to create a discipleship pathway to help people of all ages grow in faith. They explored how an intergenerational approach would strengthen faith formation. How would an intergenerational approach shape the way they sent people out from worship into day-to-day life?

After several months of exploration, their discovery was that they would seek a staff person whose responsibility was intergenerational ministry. Validation came in the form of a 17 percent increase in pledges. Of course, there were disappointments, too. Even after several months of conversation about intergenerational ministry some people didn't understand what all the exploration and discussion was about. "We don't understand how things are going to be different."

Then Lent arrived. The Lenten theme was "Go." On the Saturday after Easter, seventy-five people went out to different places in the community to serve. For example, some went to nursing homes. People who were not physically able to go out stayed at the church building and they worked on projects there. For example, one group put together snack packs for a local elementary school.

The next day, the Lord's Day, people offered testimonies about their experiences. A woman in her mid-eighties stood up and said, "We're new to this church. And I know that there's an emphasis here on intergenerational ministry. We had the privilege yesterday of working with a six year old. It was such a beautiful and fun thing to do!" Lisa, the pastor, said "Hallelujah" to herself. She thought, "Finally, someone is articulating the language we have been saying for eighteen months." Yes, testimony can be a form of validation.

A THEOLOGY OF PLENTY

What is your congregation's Exodus story? I don't mean the burning bush story. Though the experience of the fire that could not be consumed was surely one of Moses's last thoughts on earth. I'm not referring to the tribe beginning their learning journey in the desert without compass and L. L. Bean backpacks, though stealing away from Pharaoh by night and wondrously crossing the Red Sea is worthy of everyone's imagination. I'm referring to an Exodus story that I somehow missed during the first forty years of my life. The Exodus story I'm thinking of involves construction of the tabernacle. In Exodus are chapters with detailed instructions for the tabernacle's construction—an ancient version of a contemporary architect's schematic drawings. What you will find in Exodus 36 is the fund-raising effort: the collection that will make it possible to follow through on the instructions. The first move was to start with a freewill offering (anything to avoid asking friends for money). It was at least a beginning.

Yet, it turned out to be more than a beginning. What happened was that Moses asked for people to bring morning offerings, and that's exactly what they did. Except the people didn't stop. Every morning there were more offerings. The liturgical design group pulled Moses aside and said, "We have more than enough to build the sanctuary and we don't have Fort Knox for storage of the gifts. Tell them enough is enough." This would be like a rabbi announcing to the synagogue members that they need to stop their giving *right now* because the ten million received far exceeds the two million sought.

Certainly in congregational life there are experiences of scarcity. It is September and you are short three Sunday School teachers. Denominational dues are up 15 percent and the board budgeted for a 5 percent increase. It is Friday and you have not called on two nursing home residents you promised you would visit this week. Where did the time go?

Yet, your congregation has its own Exodus 36 story. You have your own story about plenty. Many of us have been taught that we learn from difficult things. We also learn from good experiences. Recall the time your congregation increased pledges by 17 percent as College Avenue United Methodist Church had. Remember the time you were planning for 250 in worship and the ushers had to put up folding chairs because 350 attended. It is likely that such experiences represent your congregation's learning something crucial about faith, life, and mission. It turns out that happiness doesn't always follow success. Research shows that happiness, satisfaction, and validation are the *precursors* to success.[7] Your congregation, as a living system of human beings, will accomplish wonderful things when there is a positive culture of validation in the faith community. Such validation is often evident after something new has been accomplished. You don't have to wait, though. There are good things going on all the time.

Your own story of plenty is validation of your efforts. When in the midst of a new congregational challenge, remind the community of past efforts where success flourished in bounteous measure. Think about the theological worldview your congregation holds. Is there room for abundance? When you talk of God, is equal time given to positive aspects of creation? Has there been a time when the positive response was so plentiful the community had to cry "uncle" because not to was to be overwhelmed by the overflowing goodness of God? Abundance is real. It isn't joined to flawed idealism. That is, abundance isn't a cognitive exercise of wishful thinking. In congregations that learn to do new things well, conversation about abundance is rooted in experience. "Remember when . . ." So, once again (and again), take the time to recall the occasions when more than enough was provided to you. This itself is a validating activity. It builds your learning muscles. Because learning muscles are strengthened by relationships, and relationships are strengthened by shared positive experiences.

RITES OF PASSAGES

Validation includes celebration, blessing, testimony, and living a theology of plenty. Observing rites of passage serve as validation, too. For example, celebrating a congregation's anniversary affirms its existence. Such a celebration reveals the key values and the essential lessons the congregation has shared through the years. In this way validation is not only a stretch stop along the learning journey. It is a destination, too.

Recall the first church I served, Bethlehem Presbyterian Church of Logansport, Indiana (the one with monthy hymn sings). This congregation was established by a preacher named Martin Post in 1841. When organized in November of that year, there were twenty-one members.

Rev. Post was successful in church planting. His family life may have been more challenging. He never had a fixed salary. The barrel of apples left at the man's porch from time to time was appreciated. Yet such an arrangement would not pass a Presbytery's Committee on Ministry nowadays. Rev. Post had seven children, two wives, and a stern gaze. In the gathering space at Bethlehem, Rev. Post's steely eyes look down at you (from a photograph) as if you were misbehaving in worship. If you were a child and he was the principal of the school (which he was for awhile), you knew Rev. Post did not suffer schoolboy or schoolgirl shenanigans.

Early on, the Bethlehem membership went by the names of Davidson, Frushour, Rodgers, Williamson, and Paschen ("not *that* kind of passion" she used to say when introduced). Most were farmers. Now, those names are still present in stories, if not in person.

It is after worship on the day of the church's 175th anniversary. Today I am a witness. About fifty people are standing in the basement waiting for the lunch prayer to be offered. The pastor asks if anyone has a story they'd like to share. Hands go up. Of course, there are plenty of stories to share.

> "I'm just grateful that we have had a place to worship and pray and learn for all these years. Years ago, my family gave the land for the manse and I can't think of a better gift that we have given as a family."
>
> "I heard the clock in the sanctuary and it reminded me of how time passes. It goes on. We're still here. For a while, yet. We don't know how long we will be able to keep doing this but nothing can take away the love, the life, the grace, the hard times, and the good times that this old building holds. If this building could speak, the mere words could not hold all the life that has been lived here and through here."
>
> "It must be back in 1960 or so. I am sitting with one of the Williamson boys. We were playing Connect the Dots on the worship bulletin. All of a

sudden I notice the silence around us. Everyone was looking at us. We must be making too much noise. In a stern voice, Rev. Vamos, standing tall on the pulpit, looks at us over his reading glasses (he was one of our favorite pastors). He says, 'When you boys are ready we will proceed with the Lord's business, but we don't want to put any undue pressure on you.'"

"My mother played the piano in worship for forty years. When she died this May I sang an old song she used to sing to me. She opened her eyes. We looked at each other. I held my breath. And then she died. At peace."

"Remember how we used to serve 1,000 people in one evening down in this basement each October at the chicken noodle dinner? Every one of those noodles was homemade."

In so many ways this congregation is invisible. On a good Sunday—a non-anniversary Sunday—there are thirty gathered for worship. As important as this congregation is to its members and their ancestors, it is not a church that is going to be featured in a story about growing congregations having solved the secret of reaching millennials. The building stands surrounded by cornfields. No McDonalds, Walgreens, or Walmarts are nearby. To describe where Bethlehem is located you'd best know how and where the crow flies. It could close tomorrow. If it does the relatives of Temperance Williamson will feel sad. But they've known sadness before. They will move on with planting corn in spring and harvesting corn in the fall. The clock in the sanctuary will go to some family. The ticktock will not stop. They'd make sure of that.

Today, on anniversary day, the church is uninvisible. It is alive in its true habitat. After 175 years, if there is one thing this church has learned to do, it is to host a gathering. The guests are called by name. Everyone of them: the pastors who stayed four years and went on to supposedly greener pastures; the great, great, great granddaughter of a founding member who drove all morning to attend the anniversary; the fifteen year old who will excuse himself politely before lunch is served to play in the high school football game held on a Sunday. The newspaper from the town sent a reporter out to interview the members; the photo from the visit is held by a thumbtack to the picture board.

Today attention must be paid. Its history is being revealed just as, before the digital age, a photograph slowly materializes in a tray of developer fluid in a darkroom. It makes no difference that this congregation no longer (did it ever?) represents the majority structure of religious practice and expression in North America. Down in the basement built partially by their own hands, for at least one more time, the invisible is unveiled. There is a silent knowing present in the room. This is not a people given to testimony. There have been tears in the night and miracles by broad daylight. But most revelations are kept close to the heart and far from the hearing of others. At most, today, the revelations are partially revealed. The photographic paper is put in the stop bath a little prematurely. No matter. That which is known by heart doesn't always need full expression. There's a reason God's creation has room for silence and imagination.

Surely, not everything needs to be spoken for meaning to be made. This church has hosted rites of passage before: baptisms, weddings, funerals, the coming and going of pastors, the celebration of improvements and additions to the building, and much more. This group had never, however, celebrated their 175th anniversary. We all know that every anniversary, every mark of time is different. So there will never be another such anniversary gathering either. Somehow, though, they learned how to do this. With only a modest remnant they turned today into a story of plenty. How? They took this approach:

Let's research the church history. Let's invite the former pastors. Should we have a guest preacher? The newspaper must know. Let's gather photos. How do we make sure no one is left out? It is okay if we don't have a budget for this. Act by act, the church revealed itself afresh. It became uninvisible for another day.

Standing before the congregation is the newly arrived pastor. She walks to the baptism font (now which family donated the baptismal as a gift?). "Beloved of God, the mercy of the Lord is from everlasting to everlasting. It cannot be contained but must be poured out." She holds a pitcher of water and pours the water into the font. "Nothing you have done, nothing you will ever do is enough to separate you from the love of God made known in Jesus Christ."

This isn't just an anniversary. The gathering isn't solely a reunion. It is an accomplishment of grace. These words—accomplishment, grace—aren't suppose to go together but in this great, humble unveiling, holy juxtapositions are at work. It is one of those accomplishments that only happens because of grace and work though afterward it feels mostly like grace—supported by a theology of plenty.

We can still do this. We must do this. We have to do this. After all, you are never too old to learn.

You know you are experiencing the validation part of a learning journey when the following occur:

- People tell you positive stories about the result and impact of the effort.
- You feel a desire to celebrate.
- You receive a thank you note from someone who has benefited from the congregation's work.
- You realize a quick "thank you" isn't enough and you write a long note of appreciation to another person.

- You notice that the number of affirmations voiced in the congregation is increasing relative to the number of complaints.

Questions to ask when you are aware of the needs and reality of validation include the following:

- What was the best moment of this project?
- How can we share this good news with others?
- What good in our life together should no longer be invisible?
- Are there natural rites of passages in our community that we could recognize or strengthen?
- What is our theology of abundance and scarcity? Where is the congruence in our espoused values about abundance and our actions? Where are there gaps?

Things you can do when in the season of validation include the following:

- Celebrate now. Don't wait.
- Offer blessings in worship, in a liturgical or worshipful context.
- Make time for personal testimony from those who aren't the formal or official leaders.
- Don't hold back affirmations because of a distorted view of religious humility. Lift up affirmation as a sign of the abundance of creation and the goodness of God.
- Don't wait for the end of a project to offer validation.

Chapter Nine

The Next Challenge

The Journey Continues

Sometime along the way we learn that graduation doesn't exist in adulthood. I know many of us have graduated from high school. You may have positive memories of college graduation: a warm May day, the rain stopping just long enough so commencement could be held outside. Your tassel falls down the front of your face. In front of you the speakers for the day take their seats. These are official rites. In the timeline of a life, graduation from school lasts for a moment and then passes. The formality of the ceremony fades. You wake up to a new day with new challenges. Beyond school age and into adulthood there is no such thing as graduation. No diploma exists that signifies you are finished learning. There is always another challenge waiting. After all, *commencement* means beginning. Until my last breath, until your last breath, there will always be another contest summoning you to learn, to grow, to be alive in a different manner.

Congregations are animated in this way. There will always be a next, new thing. There will always be a *next challenge* that is just beyond the reach of your congregation's current capacity. If there isn't a next challenge for your congregation, the reality may be that your faith community is not thriving.

Sabbath time is important for individuals. Families sometimes need to call time out on the crazy busyness of soccer, music, school, church, work, and so forth. Your congregation might benefit from a Sabbath. Your congregation may choose to move through Lent without team meetings. Or perhaps you can do without the live band for a month of Sundays; lower the decibel level with an a cappella song leader. However, these time-outs only can exist for a short season. The next challenge is waiting for you. The idea, need, possibility, problem is already present among you waiting to be explored.

143

Sabbath time, down time, is only one seventh of existence. This is for a reason. The reason is that human intention requires focus on work, on learning, on developing new capacity in order for our lives to flourish.

THERE IS ALWAYS A NEXT THING

The learning journey is a constant in your congregation. You are continually, in one form or another, defining a challenge, exploring the horizon of an idea, integrating disappointment, or receiving a discovery. These experiences lead to new possibilities. These possibilities are like tributaries that then become their own rivers forming additional tributaries.

In college, I had a professor who was a poet. He would bring his poems to class and read them to us. On the days he brought a finished poem he always looked tired—his shirt wrinkled, his hair uncombed. He carried a tall cup of coffee. You could see coffee stains on the printed poem.

He told the same story every time. He begged our pardon. He would be no good as a teacher today. The poem, that was what he wanted us to hear. Today was not the day he would introduce us to the glories of Keats or the whimsy of Dickinson. Why? Because, and he would say something like this every time, "Once I finish a poem I can't sleep because my mind is racing with the next idea. The couplets and meter are swimming away from me. I can't catch them. I'm paddling upstream." To demonstrate his point, his condition, he would not only share his finished poem, he'd also share a line or two from the new poem that had kept him up. "Just a beginning," he would say.

The phenomenon of the next thing isn't only true for the poet. It is true for all us. It is true for congregational leaders and the learning dynamics of congregations. Picture a congregation that worships in an old stone building. The building is located downtown. During the previous three years, the leaders dedicated much effort to the construction of a new building next to the sanctuary. The recently completed building exists to be a community center, so that those living near the church might have access to a variety of social services. On Friday nights after the high school football game, students gather. It is loud and it is fun. There is live music. During September, more than 150 youth bunch up in the new gymnasium on these Friday nights. If you look in the open door you will see a band setting up, a basketball game underway, hotdogs being handed out. On Tuesday morning two physician assistants check patients who don't have health insurance. Every Thursday evening a community meal is offered; it costs whatever donation you want to give. The menu varies—except that every night the cook makes three trays of lasagna. (She doesn't give out the tomato sauce recipe.) "When we're out, we're out," she says.

The congregational leaders went on a learning journey to accomplish the construction of this community center. They didn't call it a learning journey; they called it a project. They christened it a dream. The pastor called it the hardest work he had done in his life ("I don't like being told 'no,' but I know God doesn't make 'yes' easy"). Underneath the dynamics that made the endeavor a project, underneath the apparent tasks that constituted the dream, was the virtually universal structure of the learning journey.

Many years ago there was a sense of unease. *The city has forgotten us. We are an invisible zip code. There is no community center near us.*

This unease led to a desire for a neighborhood gathering place. The challenge was put as an evocative question: "What if we continue to worship here but we don't know our neighbors?"

Not one of the current leaders, clergy and laity, had led a building project. Not one had raised money beyond the annual campaign. Only a few in the congregation had experience with what is called "community ministry." Any such community engagement came through their vocations, not through volunteer services.

So the leaders started exploring options and scenarios. They started learning. The pastor talked to nonprofit leaders. Two members of the church council went to a conference about church construction projects. The business manager called on leaders in other churches who had led capital campaigns. A team met with teachers at the local university to learn how to assess community needs. The use of these resources signified more than information gathering. It was education; something new was being developed.

Of course, there was disappointment. The first time the congregation voted on the idea of a new community center it passed by only four votes. The pastor said to the church council, "It needs to be 100 percent or we aren't doing this." More work, more learning occurred. The pastor brought in a guest preacher of national note who preached a sermon that raised parishioners to their feet, crying and singing, "Hallelujah." This was their moment of revelation. We can do this. We *must* do this. The pastor had his 100 percent the next week.

There were many project management issues to address. The congregation had to let go of something while they were taking on this effort. The church stopped their food pantry ministry. This wasn't easy. It was their only community offering up to this point in time. Yet, the leaders, clergy and laity alike, trusted that something grander was waiting. It was like those times just before sunrise. Wait for it. Wait for it. There it is—the sun, now just over the horizon.

The congregation walked out into the new day ready for hard work. Designs were drawn, which took many hours with an architect. The funds were raised. An anonymous, out-of-town donor put the church over its goal at the last minute. Someone from the church met the construction crew every weekday at 7:00 a.m.

When the building was complete it was time for celebration. The guest preacher came back and preached a sermon that rang like a song. *You did it. You did it. You did it. No, I'm not telling the truth. Here's the truth: God did it through you!*

It didn't take long after the post-construction punch list was complete for the building to host the youth on Friday, the health clinic during the week, and the Thursday evening meals. The third week after the building opened the pastor counted more than four hundred different individuals walking through the door.

And by the third week there were already new challenges. Because the building was used so frequently there were additional utility costs (how did we miss that?). Keeping the new building clean required two custodians, not one (which will cost us more money). Some leaders wondered if perhaps a separate 501(c)(3) should be developed. There were more people participating in events held in the community center than people attending worship. "The tale is wagging the dog," said a council member. Were the new challenges primarily operational? Could they be solved by rearranging the budget? Or were the new challenges related to the vision held by congregational leaders? Who are we? What are our dreams? Who is our neighbor?

The completion of the new community center was not a graduation exercise for this downtown congregation. On celebration day no diploma was displayed in the sanctuary. The completion of the community center was a commencement signifying new challenges.

In your congregation there are hundreds of opportunities. Each opportunity contains a curriculum—a course of action waiting to be discovered. The most positive accomplishments of your congregation are the ones that lead to yet another challenge. If you accomplish something and it is truly over and done then perhaps the experience wasn't as fulsome as anticipated.

ALWAYS GROWING, ALWAYS LEARNING

One of the aha moments I had as a pastor was learning from Kennon Callahan that either my congregation was growing or it was declining.[1] Stable means static. Static means decline. Now such a simple statement seems obviously true. Then, for me, it was a revelation. This standard can be applied to measurable results. Are there the same number of people in worship? Are offerings about the same? Stability in these areas often foretells eventual decline. Laws of entropy are real. The things of this world move in the direction of inevitable decay.

The assertion that you are either growing or declining as a congregation refers to more than the number of attendees and income streams. Wisdom about the necessity of growth also pertains to the inner life of the congregation and its members. Are you learning? Are lives being changed? Do you see the possibilities of God more clearly?

You are the steward of the congregation you serve. As a congregational leader, your vocation includes the development of knowledge, skills, and wisdom to address the well-being of your community of faith. This never ends. Congregational learning has a "to be continued" feel. You never quite arrive at the distant horizon. There is always something left out, incomplete. The journey contains an ellipsis.

They have a full community center, with little money and a stressed staff so they started to work on their next step, which would be to . . .

There are multiple, possible learning journeys waiting for you and your congregation all the time. At any moment, multiple learning journeys are taking place. Regarding one issue, you are just beginning to define the challenge. For another you are on the verge of a discovering the direction for which you've been waiting. You may be taking on a whole new endeavor related to prayer ministry. The next day you are blessing a couple that is the first couple to go through the new marriage preparation experience. Songwriter Glen Phillips sings this in his song "There's Always More":

> There's always more
> A trace between what will be
> And what came before. [2]

What to do? In addition to other conceptual frameworks you hold for your congregation, do think of your faith community as a learning organization. Your congregation can continuously improve its capacity to address ever-increasing demands for the sake of its religious claims and commitments. Be a place that resembles Peter Senge's classic description of a learning organization—that is, be a place "where people continually expand their capacity to create the results they truly desire, where new and expansive patterns of thinking are nurtured, where collective aspiration is set free, and where people are continually learning how to learn together." [3] To achieve this, consider where your congregation is along the journey of any endeavor worth the effort of education. Think in terms of defining the challenge succinctly. Be willing to explore the horizon of possibilities with resources and learning partners. Come to terms with inevitable disappointment. Be receptive to the discovery waiting for you, taking on and letting go of activities, and validating the good that is developing before you.

If all this sounds complicated (and it can be), be the congregational leader that simplifies and clarifies complexity for others. You have this skill. After all, if you are a pastor you are trained as a pastoral theologian whose vocation is to make clearer the sometimes incomprehensible mysteries of life. Why am I here? What is life for? What does death mean?

If you are a layperson, think of the other life arenas in which your expertise places you in the clear side of complexity. You know some things deeply and unambiguously. Laity can learn as much about congregational dynamics, the mystery of the overtly religious, and the difficulty of operational necessities as they do whatever else most interests them in life. A skill that will allow you to address the constant stream of next challenges is the ability to illuminate and prioritize the challenges your faith community holds.

FIVE QUESTIONS

As you face challenge after challenge, opportunity after opportunity, the learning journey required to accomplish new things will become more evident. You will find that the gradations that lead to accomplishment become more clear-cut, more distinct. They can be simplified. For example, five key questions drive the entire journey:

- What's the challenge?
- What have we done?
- What are we learning?
- What's our next step?
- What help do we need?

No matter where you are on the journey, these questions will guide your learning.

What's the challenge? Keep this question alive. It is important to know what problem you are trying to solve. It is important to match the problem you are solving with the outside resources you are using. Just as a physician doesn't want to misdiagnose and design an intervention that is a mismatch, you want congruence between the challenge you have designed, the reality you face, and the resources you seek.

What have we done? Frequently along the way you will benefit from looking back on what you have done so far. Where you have been will guide your path ahead. Reflect on recent, past actions. Keeping track of activities locates where you are on the journey. So, for example, when your team gathers, build time into the beginning of your meeting to review what has brought you to this moment.

What are we learning? Asking what you are learning keeps in front of people that every worthwhile endeavor is a learning experience. You aren't just in the midst of accomplishing something new. You are learning to do something new. By reviewing your learning you are keeping new knowledge available to your congregation for the next challenge. Congregational learning is cumulative not episodic.

What's our next step? Such a question demonstrates bias for action. It keeps your congregation from talking too much about ideas. One way your congregation might become too stable, too static, is to talk about issues for months. It is one thing to explore thoroughly. It is another, negative reality to explore infinitely. Consistently ask, "What's our next step? What's our plan?"

What help do we need? Mastery only comes when addressing a challenge with both the congregation's ingenuity and an outside resource. The most reliable way to learn is to be an open system when seeking knowledge. Go beyond yourself. Seek help. Appreciate wise counsel. Seek knowledge that is wisely theological. Yet, also look beyond that which is strictly religious. There is much to learn from the social sciences, economics, and the arts. When it comes to learning, God does not create a chasm between the sacred and the secular. Learn from helpers who've been on the journey before you.

Being aware that there is always a next challenge is the primary step that will seal the conceptual framework of the learning journey and its accompanying behaviors in your mind. It's when you see these dynamics at work in multiple challenges that you will understand that these dynamics are apparent in almost every endeavor worth doing, in every endeavor that leads to education or transformation. Learn in community. Don't go solo. Always be looking for resources that will help you learn.

Timing is of the essence. Know that going slowly early on will make the way for moving promptly once the way is clear.

Be true to your congregation's values. Stay theologically coherent. Be trained by life. Pay attention to the rites of passages taking place in your faith community.

Remember the congregation that finished the new community center building. Near the final stages of construction, the pastor went to the head of the building team and said, "We need a cornerstone."

The team leader asked, "Why? I thought Jesus was the cornerstone."

The pastor said, "Well sure, but a cornerstone would be nice don't you think? We've accomplished a lot. It would be the finishing touch."

The team leader said, "Oh, pastor, we're not finished with this. We're only beginning."

There was no cornerstone. Which is to say there was no graduation—only commencement, only new challenges signifying greater results and more expansive impact: a congregation of God's people learning more and more each day.

You know you are facing a next challenge when the following occur:

- What you have just finished leads naturally, however unintended, to a new challenge.
- You feel tired with the thought that things aren't wrapped up and finished.
- You see the need to define a new challenge that wasn't part of the plan a year ago.
- You see a new journey of challenge to exploration through disappointment to discovery developing before you even when the way ahead isn't entirely clear.
- The affirmations and validations begin to include "I wish" or "if we had only thought of" type statements.

Questions to ask when you are aware of the needs and reality of a next challenge include the following:

- Have there been unintended consequences of our accomplishment?
- What do we need in order to have the energy and commitment to address this new challenge?
- What outside resource might be a good beginning place for us based on our current capacity?
- Does this challenge come from the organizational, life, or religious realm of our life together? Are we paying proper attention to all three realms?
- What is the cost of not addressing this new challenge soon? What is the cost of addressing this challenge right now?

Things you can do when observing the need to address a new challenge include the following:

- Work on defining the next challenge clearly and simply.
- Go ahead and seek resource help matched to your capacity and worldview.
- Share with others where you think you are on the learning journey and where you are headed.
- Make sure your relationships with key leaders are healthy.
- State what it means for you to see your congregation as a learning community.

Chapter Ten

Conclusion

Life Is for Learning

At first, they didn't have a clue. They selected leaders by casting lots (Acts 1:26). How can that be a good thing? The first Christians lacked clarity about many aspects of their life together. This was not unlike the experience of the Israelites centuries earlier, wandering in the wilderness with no sight of a promised land. The early Christians were on a learning journey within a landscape that was far and wide, with the horizon beyond reach.

They faced challenges for which they had no answers. Who was part of the community and who was not? The rules of hospitality weren't evident. When it came to serving a meal, the early followers of Christ didn't know what to do with diet restrictions. In what manner should the food be served? What *kind* of food should be offered? Who was welcome at the table? More challenges became apparent. What did it mean to share all things in common? Who should be the leader? Was circumcision necessary? How does one raise funds for the church in Jerusalem? These were all things to be learned.

Then, slowly, in a measured pace, they learned how to do new things well. They applied the teachings of Christ to the practice of hospitality; sometimes you defer your own opinion for the benefit of another. If it offends a friend to eat meat, then don't eat meat in their presence. They learned how to make the first church potluck into something like a sacrament.

If the faith community was going to survive beyond one generation, clarity as well as faith was needed. So, roles and functions were solidified for leaders. Some were deacons; some were evangelists; some were healers; others were preachers.

The first followers of Jesus Christ learned how to explore challenging aspects of their faith. Is our mission to Jews? Is our mission to Gentiles? With theological coherence they developed strategies to reach both Jews and Gentiles, resolving this previously contested issue.

These learnings didn't just happen. There were disappointments along the way (the Jerusalem church is out of money). There were epiphanies (the risen Christ appeared to Saul). We know that the learnings resulted in a sense of validation among the early Christians because their new knowledge is represented as testimony, blessing, and celebration in the New Testament. In fact, the Gospel of Matthew is taught by some scholars as a summary of the learnings and teachings represented in narrative form—a kind of curriculum for the church.[1] The Acts of the Apostles captures the early church's challenges and explorations. Some of the Epistles describe discoveries and projects taken on by the early church; they are evidence of learning journeys.

We are learning still. I sit in worship. The pastor leads us in the Lord's Prayer. She says, "Let us now pray the prayer that Jesus teaches us still." Yes, Jesus does teach us, present tense. We are in this learning community together—learning to make life better, learning to make the organization called "church" better, learning to be more true to our religious claims and commitments.

I suppose in some perfect world we wouldn't need institutions and organizations to learn. We wouldn't need buildings and budgets and board members. We wouldn't need them at all. We would only need each other and some transcendent aim. Yet, for education and transformation to occur, institutions and organizations, for all the frustration and disappointment they create, are necessary carriers of the conditions that lead to learning. On our own, we aren't sturdy enough to carry out the development needed to manage the demands of life. Structure and resources are needed for sustained learning.

Congregations support navigation of the mysteries of life, the potential of love, connection with others, sacrifice, forgiveness, transcendence, service, and so much more. Yes, other learning organizations exist, thank goodness. For all its limitations, the local congregation is a special kind of host for necessary learning. Even when the learning is about the institution itself, the one called "congregation"; the new knowledge has the potential to be the means for human flourishing and not just sustaining the status quo of a static community. The local congregation relates learning to a religious sensibility that, even in this secular age, is not going to disappear from human consciousness.[2]

Nothing just happens. Experiences represent learned behavior. It is still Sunday morning. I'm looking at the worship bulletin. The order of worship corresponds to centuries of worship theology. Each act of worship is practice for key life activities. As Geoffrey Wainwright asserts, "Worship is better seen as the point of concentration at which the whole of the Christian life comes to ritual focus."[3] The way we pray is the way we believe. You may have learned the Latin in college or seminary: *lex orandi, lex credendi.*

I learned to worship by watching others. I learned by studying. I learned by leading worship. In front of me is a six year old. Her mother holds the hymnal for her. When it comes time for the prayers (including the prayers that Jesus teaches us still), the mother takes her child's hands and places them palm up to God.

In the announcement section of the worship bulletin is information about a special class coming up about dealing with serious illness. In this Protestant church the class will be taught by a Roman Catholic laywoman.

In the bulletin is a paragraph about the stained glass window that was recently sent away and repaired; secured for another generation. Three years ago the congregation didn't know what to do with this beautiful window. They just knew if they didn't take care of it now it wouldn't be whole, present, illuminating in the future. Now the congregation has celebrated its safe return. Several leaders now know so much more about the trusteeship of historic stained glass. They learned to take care of this work of art. The images in the glass point to the mystery of the Gospel. Te Deum! To God be the Glory!

Another announcement: A new partnership with two local schools is beginning. Not too long ago a previous partnership with a school had run its life course. A new challenge—new schools, new possibilities, new learning—exists between the lines of the announcement.

There's more. In any congregation there is always more than what is apparent: a class on the Biblical scholarship of James Kugel, the blessing of the animals (have we done this before?), the flu shot clinic, prayer shawls, Godly Play, giving kiosks (how do these things work?), the Between Jobs program. All of these things began as an idea, a sense of unease, a challenge. Then, you just don't think of an idea, you discover how to make the idea a reality. You learn.

Some of the learning has to do with life. Some of the learning is explicitly about God. Some learning supports the organizational life of the congregation. The best learning is found at the intersection of all three.

Again, one more time: what challenge does your congregation face? What learning needs to take place? At this moment you may not have a clue. But soon you will. You will articulate your challenge clearly. You will move beyond disappointment. You will explore possibilities. You will discover something new about yourself and the faith community to which you belong. You will have the opportunity to feel close to God and to those with whom you are learning. You will find congruence between what you are doing, what you are learning, and your religious claims and commitments. Life is for learning, and you are part of a learning congregation.

Notes

INTRODUCTION

1. Ronald Heifetz. *Leadership Without Easy Answers.* Cambridge, MA: Harvard University Press, 1998.
2. Peter Senge. *The Fifth Discipline: The Art & Practice of the Learning Organization.* 2nd ed. New York: Doubleday/Currency, 2006, 4.
3. James Russell Lowell. "The Present Crisis." Poets.org. Accessed October 16, 2016. https://www.poets.org/poetsorg/poem/present-crisis.
4. Jonathan Sacks. "Devarim (5774)—The Leader as Teacher—Rabbi Sacks." Rabbisacks.org, April 4, 2016. Accessed October 16, 2016. http://www.rabbisacks.org/devarim-5774-leader-teacher/.
5. Robert Kegan and Lisa Laskow Lahey. *How the Way We Talk Can Change the Way We Work: Seven Languages for Transformation.* San Francisco: Jossey-Bass, 2001.
6. Ibid., 67–71.

1. THE JOURNEY

1. Robert Kegan. *In Over Our Heads: The Mental Demands of Modern Life.* Cambridge, MA: Harvard University Press, 1994, 164.
2. Cynthia Bourgeault. *Centering Prayer and Inner Awakening.* Cambridge, MA: Cowley Publications, 2004.
3. William R. Duggan. *Strategic Intuition: The Creative Spark in Human Achievement.* New York: Columbia University Press, 2007, 1–6. Duggan describes how strategic intuition is different from flash judgment.
4. Peter M. Senge. *The Fifth Discipline: The Art and Practice of the Learning Organization.* New York: Doubleday/Currency, 2006.
5. Joseph Campbell. *The Hero with a Thousand Faces.* 3rd ed. Novato, CA: New World Library, 2008.
6. James E. Loder. *The Transforming Moment.* Colorado Springs: Helmers & Howard, 1989.
7. James E. Loder. *The Logic of the Spirit: Human Development in Theological Perspective.* San Francisco: Jossey-Bass, 1998.

2. GETTING THE HELP YOU DESERVE

1. Sonja J. Stewart and Jerome W. Berryman. *Young Children and Worship.* Louisville, KY: Westminster John Knox Press, 1989.

2. Jerome W. Berryman. *Godly Play: An Imaginative Approach to Religious Education.* Minneapolis, MN: Augsburg Fortress, 1995.

3. G. W. Allport. *Personality: A Psychological Interpretation.* New York: Henry Holt, 1937.

4. Antoine de Saint-Exupéry and Richard Howard. *The Little Prince.* San Diego: Harcourt, 2000, 60.

5. American Psychiatric Association. *Diagnostic and Statistical Manual of Mental Disorders (DSM-5), Fifth Edition.* Arlington, VA: American Psychiatric Association, 2013.

6. Bettina Bergo. "Emmanuel Levinas." Stanford Encyclopedia of Philosophy Archive, first published July 23, 2006; substantive revision August 3, 2011. Accessed October 22, 2016. https://plato.stanford.edu/archives/sum2015/entries/levinas/.

7. John S. McClure. *Other-Wise Preaching: A Postmodern Ethic for Homiletics.* St. Louis, MO: Chalice Press, 2001, 11.

8. Union of Reform Judaism (URJ). *Strengthening Congregations: Paving the Road to Meaningful Young Adult Engagement: A Report from the 2013–2014 Young Adult Engagement Community of Practice.* Accessed October 22, 2016. http://www.urj.org/sites/default/files/YoungAdultEngagementResource.pdf.

9. Edwin H. Friedman. *Generation to Generation: Family Process in Church and Synagogue.* New York: Guilford Press, 1985.

10. Robert Kegan and Lisa Laskow Lahey. *Immunity to Change: How to Overcome It and Unlock Potential in Yourself and Your Organization.* Boston: Harvard Business Press, 2009. The authors describe ways for a learner to be the subject of their challenge, to hold the challenge, rather than the challenge having a hold on them. Their developmental theory informs various aspects of this work related to congregations.

11. Ibid., 76.

12. Robert Kegan. *In Over Our Heads: The Mental Demands of Modern Life.* Cambridge, MA: Harvard University Press, 1994, 32.

13. Kegan and Lahey. 28.

14. Kegan, 32.

15. Abraham H. Maslow. *A Theory of Human Motivation.* Reprint ed. Eastford, CT: Martino Fine Books, 2013.

3. CHALLENGE

1. Jerome E. Groopman. *How Doctors Think.* Boston: Houghton Mifflin, 2007, 17.

2. Ibid., 24.

3. John P. Kotter. *A Sense of Urgency.* Boston: Harvard Business Press, 2008.

4. "Summarizing the Law." American Bible Society: Resources. Accessed October 22, 2016. http://bibleresources.americanbible.org/resource/summarizing-the-law.

5. Fred Rogers. *You Are Special: Words of Wisdom for All Ages from a Beloved Neighbor.* New York: Penguin Books, 1995, 115.

6. Melissa Armstrong-Hansche and Neil MacQueen. *Workshop Rotation: A New Model for Sunday School.* Louisville, KY: Geneva Press, 2000.

4. EXPLORATION

1. Jane Thibault and Richard Lyon Morgan. *Pilgrimage into the Last Third of Life: 7 Gateways to Spiritual Growth*. Nashville, TN: Upper Room Books, 2012.

2. Dorothy C. Bass, Kathleen A. Cahalan, Bonnie J. Miller-McLemore, James R. Nieman, and Christian B. Scharen. *Christian Practical Wisdom: What It Is, Why It Matters*. Grand Rapids, MI: Eerdmans, 2016, 1–15.

3. Ibid.

4. William Stafford. *Ask Me: 100 Essential Poems*. Minneapolis, MN: Graywolf Press, 2014, 16.

5. Richard Linklater and Kim Krizan. *Before Sunrise*. Accessed October 22, 2016. https://indiegroundfilms.files.wordpress.com/2014/01/before-sunrise-numbered.pdf, 63.

6. Ibid.

7. Parker J. Palmer. *A Hidden Wholeness: The Journey toward an Undivided Life: Welcoming the Soul and Weaving Community in a Wounded World*. San Francisco: Jossey-Bass, 2004, 132.

5. DISAPPOINTMENT

1. Craig Dykstra. *Growing in the Life of Faith: Education and Christian Practices*. Louisville, KY: Westminster John Knox Press, 1999, 21.

2. Sigmund Freud and Josef Breuer. *Studies in Hysteria*. Translated by Nicola Luckhurst. London: Penguin Books, 2004, 306.

3. Gary Klein. *Intuition at Work: Why Developing Your Gut Instincts Will Make You Better at What You Do*. New York: Currency/Doubleday, 2003, 88–91.

4. W. Paul Jones. *Worlds Within a Congregation: Dealing with Theological Diversity*. Nashville: Abingdon Press, 2000.

5. Ibid., 94.

6. Burton Z. Cooper and John S. McClure. *Claiming Theology in the Pulpit*. Louisville, KY: Westminster John Knox Press, 2003.

7. Ibid., 135–42.

8. Sonja M. Stewart and Jerome Berryman. *Young Children and Worship*. Louisville, KY: Westminster John Knox Press, 1989.

9. E. C. Bentley. *Trent's Last Case*. Mineola, NY: Dover Publications, 1997, 1.

10. Henry Cloud and John Townsend. "What Is Good Christian Therapy?" Cloud-Townsend Resources. July 25, 2009. Accessed October 22, 2016. http://www.cloudtownsend.com/christian-therapy/.

6. DISCOVERY

1. John Kounios and Mark Beeman. *The Eureka Factor: Aha Moments, Creative Insight, and the Brain*. New York: Random House, 2015, 27–28. As you might imagine, there are many versions of the Archimedes story. The version recounted in the book by Kounios and Beeman is a good one.

2. William H. Willimon. *Sunday Dinner: The Lord's Supper and the Christian Life*. Nashville, TN: Upper Room, 1998.

3. Christian Madsbjerg and Mikkel B. Rasmussen. *The Moment of Clarity: Using the Human Sciences to Solve Your Toughest Business Problems*. Boston: Harvard Business Review Press, 2014.

4. George Hunsinger. *Disruptive Grace: Studies in the Theology of Karl Barth*. Grand Rapids, MI: William B. Eerdmans Publishing, 2000, 16.

5. John Dominic Crossan. *Finding Is the First Act: Trove Folktales and Jesus' Treasure Parable*. Eugene, OR: Wipf & Stock, 2008.

6. Luther K. Snow. *The Power of Asset Mapping: How Your Congregation Can Act on Its Gifts*. Lanham, MD: Rowman & Littlefield, 2004.

7. James C. Collins and Jerry L. Porras. *Built to Last: Successful Habits of Visionary Companies*. 10th ed. New York: HarperBusiness: 2004.

7. TAKING ON AND LETTING GO

1. Aristotle, W. D. Ross, and Lesley Brown. *The Nicomachean Ethics*. Oxford: Oxford University Press, 2009, 23.

2. Gary Klein. "Flexecution as a Paradigm for Replanning, Part 1." *IEEE Intelligent Systems* 22, no. 5 (2007): 79–83. doi:10.1109/mis.2007.4338498.

3. Gary Klein. "Flexecution, Part 2: Understanding and Supporting Flexible Execution." *IEEE Intelligent Systems* 22, no. 6 (2007): 108. doi:10.1109/mis.2007.107.

4. Hillary Rodham Clinton. *It Takes a Village: And Other Lessons Children Teach Us*. New York: Simon & Schuster, 2006.

5. Don C. Dinkmeyer, and Gary D. McKay. *The Parent's Handbook: Systematic Training for Effective Parenting*. Bowling Green, KY: STEP Publishers, 1997.

6. Kathleen A. Cahalan. *Projects That Matter: Successful Planning & Evaluation for Religious Organizations*. Lanham, MD: Rowman & Littlefield, 2003, 16.

7. Ibid., 17.

8. Essie Kathryn Scott Payne. *Mama and the Hills of Home: My Spiritual Pillars*. Berkeley, CA: Creative Arts Book, 2002, 46.

9. Daniel Siegel. *The Developing Mind: How Relationships and the Brain Shape Who We Are*. 2nd ed. New York: Guilford Press, 45.

10. Mike Redmond. "Money and Faith: William G. Enright and the Big American Taboo." Faith and Leadership. January 23, 2014. Accessed October 23, 2016. https://www.faithandleadership.com/money-and-faith-william-g-enright-and-big-american-taboo.

11. Dorothy C. Bass, Kathleen A. Cahalan, Bonnie J. Miller-McLemore, James R. Nieman, and Christian B. Scharen. *Christian Practical Wisdom: What It Is, Why It Matters*. Grand Rapids, MI: Eerdmans, 2016.

8. VALIDATION

1. Arthur Miller. *Death of a Salesman*. Edited by Gerald Clifford Weales. New York: Penguin Books, 1996, 56.

2. Robert Kegan and Lisa Laskow Lahey. *How the Way We Talk Can Change the Way We Work: Seven Languages for Transformation*. San Francisco: Jossey-Bass, 2001, 13–32.

3. Robert D. Lupton. *Toxic Charity: How Churches and Charities Hurt Those They Help (and How to Reverse It)*. New York: HarperOne, 2011.

4. John Mordechai Gottman, Julie Schwartz Gottman, and Joan DeClaire. *10 Lessons to Transform Your Marriage: America's Love Lab Experts Share Their Strategies for Strengthening Your Relationship*. New York: Three Rivers Press, 2007, 4.

5. Lawrence A. Hoffman. *The Way into Jewish Prayer*. Woodstock, VT: Jewish Lights Publishing, 2000, 30.

6. John Trent and Gary Smalley. *The Blessing: Giving the Gift of Unconditional Love and Acceptance*. Updated ed. Nashville, TN: Thomas Nelson, 2011, 115–32.

7. Shawn Achor. *The Happiness Advantage: The Seven Principles that Fuel Success and Performance at Work*. London: Virgin, 2011.

9. THE NEXT CHALLENGE

1. Kennon L. Callahan. *Twelve Keys to an Effective Church*. San Francisco: Jossey-Bass, 1997, xxv.
2. Glen Phillips. "Lyrics—Glen Phillips." Accessed October 26, 2016. http://www.glenphillips.com/lyrics/.
3. Peter M. Senge. *The Fifth Discipline: The Art and Practice of the Learning Organization*. 2nd ed. New York: Doubleday/Currency, 2006, 3.

10. CONCLUSION

1. Alan J. P. Garrow. *The Gospel of Matthew's Dependence on the "Didache."* London: T & T Clark, 2004.
2. Charles Taylor. *A Secular Age*. Cambridge, MA: Belknap Press of Harvard University Press, 2007.
3. Geoffrey Wainwright. *Doxology: The Praise of God in Worship, Doctrine, and Life: A Systematic Theology*. New York: Oxford University Press, 1984, 8.

Index

161

Bibliography

Achor, Shawn. *The Happiness Advantage: The Seven Principles that Fuel Success and Performance at Work*. London: Virgin, 2011.

Allport, G. W. *Personality: A Psychological Interpretation*. New York: Henry Holt, 1937.

American Psychiatric Association. *Diagnostic and Statistical Manual of Mental Disorders (DSM-5), Fifth Edition*. Arlington, VA: American Psychiatric Association, 2013.

Aristotle, W. D. Ross, and Lesley Brown. *The Nicomachean Ethics*. Oxford: Oxford University Press, 2009.

Armstrong-Hansche, Melissa, and Neil MacQueen. *Workshop Rotation: A New Model for Sunday School*. Louisville, KY: Geneva Press, 2000.

Bass, Dorothy C., Kathleen A. Cahalan, Bonnie J. Miller-McLemore, James R. Nieman, and Christian B. Scharen. *Christian Practical Wisdom: What It Is, Why It Matters*. Grand Rapids, MI: Eerdmans, 2016.

Bentley, E. C. *Trent's Last Case*. Mineola, NY: Dover Publications, 1997.

Bergo, Bettina. "Emmanuel Levinas." Stanford Encyclopedia of Philosophy Archive. First published July 23, 2006; substantive revision August 3, 2011. Accessed October 22, 2016. http://plato.stanford.edu/archives/sum2015/entries/levinas/.

Berryman, Jerome W. *Godly Play: An Imaginative Approach to Religious Education*. Minneapolis, MN: Augsburg Fortress, 1995.

Bourgeault, Cynthia. *Centering Prayer and Inner Awakening*. Cambridge, MA: Cowley Publications, 2004.

Cahalan, Kathleen A. *Projects That Matter: Successful Planning & Evaluation for Religious Organizations*. Lanham, MD: Rowman & Littlefield, 2003.

Callahan, Kennon L. *Twelve Keys to an Effective Church*. San Francisco: Jossey-Bass, 1997.

Campbell, Joseph. *The Hero with a Thousand Faces*. 3rd ed. Novato, CA: New World Library, 2008.

Clinton, Hillary Rodham. *It Takes a Village: And Other Lessons Children Teach Us*. New York: Simon & Schuster, 2006.

Cloud, Henry, and John Townsend. "What Is Good Christian Therapy?" Cloud-Townsend Resources. July 25, 2009. Accessed October 22, 2016. http://www.cloudtownsend.com/christian-therapy/.

Collins, James C., and Jerry I. Porras. *Built to Last: Successful Habits of Visionary Companies*. 10th ed. New York: HarperBusiness, 2004.

Cooper, Burton Z., and John S. McClure. *Claiming Theology in the Pulpit*. Louisville, KY: Westminster John Knox Press, 2003.

Crossan, John Dominic. *Finding Is the First Act: Trove Folktales and Jesus' Treasure Parable*. Eugene, OR: Wipf & Stock, 2008.

Dinkmeyer, Don C., and Gary D. McKay. *The Parent's Handbook: Systematic Training for Effective Parenting*. Bowling Green, KY: STEP Publishers, 1997.

Duggan, William R. *Strategic Intuition: The Creative Spark in Human Achievement*. New York: Columbia University Press, 2007.

Dykstra, Craig. *Growing in the Life of Faith: Education and Christian Practices*. Louisville, KY: Westminster John Knox Press, 1999.

Freud, Sigmund, and Josef Breuer. *Studies in Hysteria*. Translated by Nicola Luckhurst. London: Penguin Books, 2004.

Friedman, Edwin H. *Generation to Generation: Family Process in Church and Synagogue*. New York: Guilford Press, 1985.

Garrow, Alan J. P. *The Gospel of Matthew's Dependence on the "Didache."* London: T & T Clark, 2004.

Gottman, John Mordechai, Julie Schwartz Gottman, and Joan DeClaire. *10 Lessons to Transform Your Marriage: America's Love Lab Experts Share Their Strategies for Strengthening Your Relationship*. New York: Three Rivers Press, 2007.

Groopman, Jerome E. *How Doctors Think*. Boston: Houghton Mifflin, 2007.

Heifetz, Ronald A. *Leadership Without Easy Answers*. Cambridge, MA: Harvard University Press, 1998.

Hoffman, Lawrence A. *The Way into Jewish Prayer*. Woodstock, VT: Jewish Lights Publishing, 2000.

Holy Bible: NRSV, New Revised Standard Version. New York: Harper Bibles, 2007.

Hunsinger, George. *Disruptive Grace: Studies in the Theology of Karl Barth*. Grand Rapids, MI: William B. Eerdmans Publishing, 2000.

Jones, W. Paul. *Worlds Within a Congregation: Dealing with Theological Diversity*. Nashville: Abingdon Press, 2000.

Kegan, Robert. *In Over Our Heads: The Mental Demands of Modern Life*. Cambridge, MA: Harvard University Press, 1994.

Kegan, Robert, and Lisa Laskow Lahey. *How the Way We Talk Can Change the Way We Work: Seven Languages for Transformation*. San Francisco: Jossey-Bass, 2001.

———. *Immunity to Change: How to Overcome It and Unlock Potential in Yourself and Your Organization*. Boston: Harvard Business Press, 2009.

Klein, Gary. *Intuition at Work: Why Developing Your Gut Instincts Will Make You Better at What You Do*. New York: Currency/Doubleday, 2003.

———. "Flexecution as a Paradigm for Replanning, Part 1." *IEEE Intelligent Systems* 22, no. 5 (2007): 79–83. doi:10.1109/mis.2007.4338498.

———. "Flexecution, Part 2: Understanding and Supporting Flexible Execution." *IEEE Intelligent Systems* 22, no. 6 (2007): 108–12. doi:10.1109/mis.2007.107.

Kotter, John P. *A Sense of Urgency*. Boston: Harvard Business Press, 2008.

Kounios, John, and Mark Beeman. *The Eureka Factor: Aha Moments, Creative Insight, and the Brain*. New York: Random House, 2015.

Linklater, Richard, and Kim Krizan. *Before Sunrise*. Accessed October 22, 2016. https://indiegroundfilms.files.wordpress.com/2014/01/before-sunrise-numbered.pdf.

Loder, James E. *The Logic of the Spirit: Human Development in Theological Perspective*. San Francisco: Jossey-Bass, 1998.

———. *The Transforming Moment*. Colorado Springs: Helmers & Howard, 1989.

Lowell, James Russell. "The Present Crisis." Poets.org. Accessed October 16, 2016. https://www.poets.org/poetsorg/poem/present-crisis.

Lupton, Robert D. *Toxic Charity: How Churches and Charities Hurt Those They Help (and How to Reverse It)*. New York: HarperOne, 2011.

Madsbjerg, Christian, and Mikkel B. Rasmussen. *The Moment of Clarity: Using the Human Sciences to Solve Your Toughest Business Problems*. Boston: Harvard Business Review Press, 2014.

Maslow, Abraham H. *A Theory of Human Motivation*. Reprint ed. Eastford, CT: Martino Fine Books, 2013.

McClure, John S. *Other-Wise Preaching: A Postmodern Ethic for Homiletics*. St. Louis, MO: Chalice Press, 2001.

Miller, Arthur. *Death of a Salesman*. Edited by Gerald Clifford Weales. New York: Penguin Books, 1996.

Redmond, Mike. "Money and Faith: William G. Enright and the Big American Taboo." Faith and Leadership. January 23, 2014. Accessed October 23, 2016. https://www.faithandleadership.com/money-and-faith-william-g-enright-and-big-american-taboo.

Palmer, Parker J. *A Hidden Wholeness: The Journey toward an Undivided Life: Welcoming the Soul and Weaving Community in a Wounded World*. San Francisco: Jossey-Bass, 2004.

Payne, Essie Kathryn Scott. *Mama and the Hills of Home: My Spiritual Pillars*. Berkeley, CA: Creative Arts Book, 2002.

Phillips, Glen. "Lyrics—Glen Phillips." Accessed October 26, 2016. http://www.glenphillips.com/lyrics/.

Rogers, Fred. *You Are Special: Words of Wisdom for All Ages from a Beloved Neighbor*. New York: Penguin Books, 1995.

Sacks, Jonathan. "Devarim (5774)—The Leader as Teacher—Rabbi Sacks." Rabbisacks.org. April 4, 2016. Accessed October 16, 2016. http://www.rabbisacks.org/devarim-5774-leader-teacher/.

Saint-Exupéry, Antoine de, and Richard Howard. *The Little Prince*. San Diego: Harcourt, 2000.

Senge, Peter M. *The Fifth Discipline: The Art and Practice of the Learning Organization*. 2nd ed. New York: Doubleday/Currency, 2006.

Siegel, Daniel. *The Developing Mind: How Relationships and the Brain Shape Who We Are*. 2nd ed. New York: Guilford Press, 2012.

Snow, Luther K. *The Power of Asset Mapping: How Your Congregation Can Act on Its Gifts*. Lanham, MD: Rowman & Littlefield, 2004.

Stafford, William. *Ask Me: 100 Essential Poems*. Minneapolis, MN: Graywolf Press, 2014.

Stewart, Sonja M., and Jerome Berryman. *Young Children and Worship*. Louisville, KY: Westminster John Knox Press, 1989.

"Summarizing the Law." American Bible Society: Resources. Accessed October 22, 2016. http://bibleresources.americanbible.org/resource/summarizing-the-law.

Taylor, Charles. *A Secular Age*. Cambridge, MA: Belknap Press of Harvard University Press, 2007.

Thibault, Jane M., and Richard Lyon Morgan. *Pilgrimage into the Last Third of Life: 7 Gateways to Spiritual Growth*. Nashville, TN: Upper Room, 2012.

Trent, John, and Gary Smalley. *The Blessing: Giving the Gift of Unconditional Love and Acceptance*. Updated ed. Nashville, TN: Thomas Nelson, 2011.

Union of Reform Judaism (URJ). *Strengthening Congregations: Paving the Road to Meaningful Young Adult Engagement: A Report from the 2013–2014 Young Adult Engagement Community of Practice*. Accessed October 22, 2016. http://www.urj.org/sites/default/files/YoungAdultEngagementResource.pdf.

Wainwright, Geoffrey. *Doxology: The Praise of God in Worship, Doctrine, and Life: A Systematic Theology*. New York: Oxford University Press, 1984.

Willimon, William H. *Sunday Dinner: The Lord's Supper and the Christian Life*. Nashville, TN: Upper Room, 1998.